Angel
Miracles

*Inspirational True Stories
of Heavenly Help*

Brad Steiger &
Sherry Hansen Steiger

Avon, Massachusetts

Published by
Adams Media, an F+W Publications Company
57 Littlefield Street, Avon, MA 02322 U.S.A.
www.adamsmedia.com

ISBN-10: 1-59869-609-2
ISBN-13: 978-1-59869-609-7
Printed in the United States of America.

J I H G F E D C B A

Library of Congress Cataloging-in-Publication Data
available from publisher.

This publication is designed to provide accurate and authoritative information with
regard to the subject matter covered. It is sold with the understanding that the publisher
is not engaged in rendering legal, accounting, or other professional advice. If legal advice
or other expert assistance is required, the services of a competent professional person
should be sought.
—From a *Declaration of Principles* jointly adopted by a Committee of the
American Bar Association and a Committee of Publishers and Associations

Many of the designations used by manufacturers and sellers to distinguish their prod-
ucts are claimed as trademarks. Where those designations appear in this book and
Adams Media was aware of a trademark claim, the designations have been printed
with initial capital letters.

While all the events and experiences recounted in this book are true and happened
to real people, some of the names, dates, and places have been changed in order to
protect the privacy of certain individuals.

This book is available at quantity discounts for bulk purchases.
For information, please call 1-800-289-0963.

Introduction

*Y*es, we believe in angels—and we are not alone.

According to a poll conducted by *Time* magazine, 69 percent of Americans believe in the existence of angels, and 46 percent are certain that they have their own guardian angels to watch over them. Of those men and women polled by the newsmagazine, 32 percent claim that they have personally felt the presence and or guidance of ethereal entities in their lives.

Other polls had similar findings:

A poll conducted by *Self* magazine found that 87 percent of their readers believed in angels.

The Leger Marketing Survey of Canadians indicated that 57.1 percent of the population of Canada believes in angels.

Scripps Howard News Service released their findings that one out of every five Americans believes he or she has seen an angel or knows someone who has.

A Gallup Poll stated that 72 percent of Americans believed in angels, compared to 96 percent who believed in God, and 90 percent who believed in heaven.

A FOX News poll found that 79 percent of Americans accepted the existence of angels.

The Harris Poll declared that 68 percent of Americans believed in an angelic guardian.

An Associated Press survey stated that 97 percent of evangelical Christians counted on their angels to guide them in life. The same AP poll revealed that even among individuals without any religious affiliation, more than 50 percent believed in angels. Among the general population, 81 percent acknowledged the existence of angels.

Since 1968, we have been distributing the *Steiger Questionnaire of Mystical and Paranormal Experiences* to our readers and lecture audiences. Of the more than 30,000 respondents, 78 percent claim to have witnessed angelic activity on Earth; 89 percent believe that they have personally interacted with a guardian angel or spirit guide; and 77 percent say that they have had an encounter with a benevolent being of light. Our respondents generally describe the beings as beautiful of countenance and often majestic and awesome. Manifestations of light often accompany the heavenly beings, adding to the grandeur of their appearance and the feeling of profound reverence that suffuses those who encounter them.

The broadest definition of an angel is simply one who serves as a messenger of God. In this sense, a living person could certainly serve in such a capacity and serve God's purpose by delivering a particular thought, knowledge, or counsel that one might require at a certain crisis point. Many of us have been privileged to have a good friend or family member become an "angel" when we really needed the unconditional love and assistance of another, and some of us may even have had such a person assume a protective, "guardian angel" role for a time. However, when we speak of our true guardian angels, we are referring to those unseen, benevolent entities who, according to many traditions, have been assigned to us at birth to guide, direct us, and on occasion, to protect us.

Some skeptical psychologists and other researchers have suggested that those individuals who believe in a guiding and protective angel may be accessing an as-yet-little-known power of the mind, which enables one's subjective level of consciousness to dramatize another personality, complete with a full range of personal characteristics and its own voice. Such a theory sounds too much like a description of mental illness to those men and women who are convinced beyond reasonable doubt that they were guided, directed, and protected by a spiritual being. Those who believe completely, without question, that they interacted with a guardian angel stoutly maintain that the reality of a spiritual guide or teacher is so much more than any kind of psychological phenomenon.

The idea of a spirit guide or guardian angel dates back to the farthest reaches of antiquity. It is unlikely that anthropologists have ever discovered a single aboriginal culture that did not include the concept of a spirit guide in its theology.

All the great world religions have some kind of tradition of a guardian angel or spiritual guide assigned to each individual human soul. The ancient teachings are also in agreement that angels are an earlier and separate order of creation from that of human beings, who were sculpted from the dust of the earth, and who were brought into being a little lower in the hierarchy than the angels.

As early as the third millennium B.C.E., the written records of ancient Egypt and Mesopotamia recognized a hierarchy of supernatural beings that ruled over various parts of the Earth, the universe, and the lives of human beings. The Mesopotamians wanted to be certain that they were well protected by their spiritual guardians, the *shedu* and the *lamassu*.

In the Sanskrit texts of the ancient *Vedas*, the word for angel is *angira*; in Hebrew, *malakh*, meaning "messenger," or *bene elohim*, for "God's children"; in

Arabic, *malakah*; and in India, multiwinged angels or beings are called *garudas*. The teachings of Islam state that there are three distinct species of intelligent beings in the universe. First are the angels that are a high order of beings created of Light, the *malakh*; second, the *al-jinn*, ethereal, perhaps even multidimensional entities; and then human beings, fashioned out of the stuff of Earth and born into physical bodies. On occasion, the al-jinn can serve as helpful guides or guardians, but they can also be tricksters.

The scriptures of all the world's major faiths state firmly that angelic beings are not to be worshipped or held as objects of veneration. Even though possessed with ethereal energy and certain powers beyond those of humans, the angels are by no means omnipresent, omnipotent, or omniscient, and neither are they immune from falling into temptation or error.

In addition to their task as guardians, the merciful companions have the task of guiding their humans toward spiritual awareness. As well as being assigned to be available on occasion to give humans a helping hand, it is an integral part of their terrestrial task to lead their human wards to a clearer understanding of their true role in the cosmic scheme of things.

On December 12, 2000, the *Times* of London reported on a two-year study of the phenomenon of guardian angels conducted by Emma Heathcote, a Birmingham University Researcher. Heathcote's study, one of the first academic research projects on the subject of angels, examined the stories of over 800 Britons who claimed encounters with heavenly beings. Almost a third of those who contacted the researcher reported seeing a traditional angel with white gown and wings. Another 21 percent saw their guardian angel in human form. Others experienced the sensation of a force around them or a being engulfed in light.

Witnesses of angelic activity told Heathcote stories of seeing guardian angels at hospital beds and deathbeds, ministering to the ill or manifesting to escort souls to Heaven. A good number of accounts reported the appearance of majestic beings to allay people's fears, to let them know that they were not alone in dangerous or stressful situations.

Some scientists have suggested that such mystical experiences can be explained in terms of neural transmitters, neural networks, and brain chemistry. Rather than external entities presenting themselves to provide assurance of a celestial helping hand, psychotherapist Dr. Susan Blackmore theorizes that angel sightings are merely apparitions created by the brain in times of crisis in order to provide comfort. She believes that the feeling of transcendence that mystics describe could be the result of decreased activity in the brain's parietal lobe, which helps regulate the sense of self and physical orientation, and that perhaps the human brain is wired for mystical experiences.

While the physical activity of the brain and its psychological state may sometimes serve as a conduit to a transcendent world, we believe that the appearance of the benevolent beings that we recognize as angels is far more than a manifestation of a belief in the unknown, a blending of brain chemistry, or a personification of our hope in a spiritual comforter. We believe that there is some spiritual reality that exists outside of us, that is interested in our human condition, and with which we may somehow communicate.

One of the more dramatic accounts in Heathcote's research was an instance in which an angel appeared during a baptism at a village church in Hertfordshire in front of thirty witnesses, including the rector, churchwarden, and organist. Before the font suddenly appeared "a man, but he was totally different from the rest of us. He was wearing something long, like a robe, but it was so white it was almost transparent."

The angelic figure didn't have wings, and he simply stood there silently, looking at those assembled for the baptismal service. Children came forward with their mouths open. In a few seconds the angel was gone, but the rector stated that the appearance of the angel had changed the lives of everyone present that day.

"I interviewed a lot of people about that angel," Heathcote said, "and and everybody told the same story. Their descriptions were totally consistent."

We personally doubt that any human has ever seen angelic beings as they appear to one another in their heavenly dimensions. For one thing, angels are spiritual, rather than physical, entities. Throughout our many years of research and our interviews with hundreds of men and women from cultures and countries around the world who have claimed angelic contact, it has seemed to us that the angels have always manifested to individuals in a form that is most acceptable to him or her.

In the many cases that we have investigated, we came to believe long ago that the physical appearance of the manifesting angels depends almost completely upon the witnesses' personal cosmology—that is, their religious background, their cultural biases, and their level of spiritual evolution. Therefore, even in this technological, scientific age, a person of a conservative or fundamental religious persuasion may tend to behold angels in their traditional winged and robed persona while a member of a more liberal religious expression may be more likely to perceive an angel minus the wings and other sacerdotal trappings. On the other hand, even those who consider themselves avant-garde in many areas of contemporary life may still cherish the traditional and comforting angelic images.

Throughout the years of our research, we have continued to be impressed by the remarkable adaptability of the angel guardians. In one instance, they are the firemen who carried smoke-inhalation victims to safety and who later couldn't be found to be thanked. In another situation, a guardian angel became the traffic cop who prevented a fender-bender during rush hour from becoming a twelve-car pileup with inevitable casualties and fatalities—and who then, literally, disappeared before the real officers arrived on the scene. Sometimes they are ordinary men and women who just happened to be present at the right time to listen with an attentive ear and to relay the necessary words of advice to prevent a troubled soul from taking his or her own life.

Of one thing we are certain: If an angel should appear to you, you will perceive the heavenly messenger in an image and demeanor that will be most acceptable and understandable to you.

—*Brad Steiger*
—*Sherry Steiger*

*M*artin, a public relations manager for an Albany company, was driving on snowy New York roads shortly before Thanksgiving in 2003. As he drove toward Buffalo, the weather worsened into blizzard conditions and the highway became slick and treacherous.

Visibility became nearly zero, but Martin could make out the dark image of a large tractor-trailer looming in his rearview mirror. In spite of the slippery road, the high winds, and the swirling snow, the truck driver obviously intended to pass Martin's car. As the strong wind pushed the trailer on the ice, the mammoth vehicle repeatedly edged over into Martin's lane. Just ahead of them were the concrete walls of an underpass. With the truck encroaching more and more in his lane, Martin could see that there would not be enough room for both vehicles in the tunnel.

Martin remembers that at first he surrendered to feelings of utter helplessness, and accepted the grim reality that he might die in the next few moments. There was no time to hit the brakes: to do so would surely cause him to spin out of control and most likely swerve into the truck or the concrete embankment. There was nothing Martin could do but drive straight ahead and hope that the two vehicles could pass through the tunnel without colliding.

Then, more out of reflex than spiritual impetus, he began to recite the Twenty-Third Psalm, "Yea, though I walk through the valley of Death, thou art with me . . . ."

That was when Martin saw the angel appear between his automobile and the huge tractor-trailer. "He was incredibly large," he said. "He was surrounded by a brilliant golden light, and his wings must have stretched out for ten or twelve feet on either side of him. As I watched completely awestruck, the big angel placed one hand against the trailer and another against my car's roof—and he pushed the trailer far enough over into its lane to give both vehicles plenty of room to enter and to emerge safely from the tunnel."

Once through the underpass, Martin had to risk sliding into a ditch and pull over on the side of the road to regain his equilibrium. "I had been saved from what appeared to be almost certain death or injury by an angel," he said. "I had seen—I feel I should say beheld—an actual angel. I began to weep. I was forty-eight years old, and the only time I even thought about angels was at Christmastime. As a little kid, my mother always told me that I had a guardian angel, but I had never hoped to see him. I've been in a number of tough scrapes in my life, but this was the nearest I had ever come to dying. To be able to push apart a huge tractor-trailer and a car, that angel certainly had to have supernatural strength."

Martin said that on that most remarkable day, he learned that not only did he have a very strong and effective guardian angel, he had witnessed a wonderful demonstration of the power of prayer.

*L*auren tells the story of an angel miracle that saved her son from death or horrible injury when he was two years old.

In 1998, Lauren, her husband Patrick, and her son Jason were living in a second-story apartment in Oregon. It was a Saturday, and the family was enjoying some together time. Patrick was a long-haul truck driver who was not regularly home, and he and Jason were making up for lost time.

"Patrick was giving Jason piggyback rides in our upstairs bedroom," Lauren said. "It was a very warm day, and we had the large window next to the bed wide open. Jason got up on the bed so he could more easily climb up on his daddy's back when Patrick knelt down."

As Jason mounted his father's back, Patrick stood up, his back facing the window, and raised his leg to step over the corner of the bed so they might continue their ride. As Patrick swung around, Jason lost his grip around his daddy's neck and fell against the window screen. Patrick watched in horror as the screen gave way and Jason fell out of the window.

Lauren was putting on makeup in the bathroom when Jason fell out of the window.

"I was no more than ten feet away," she said, "but when Patrick said that Jason had fallen out of the window, I was at first uncertain whether or not he was joking, because his voice sounded so quiet and calm. Then I heard Jason crying from outside. I snapped into action and called 911."

The medics and aid car were there within minutes. Lauren lay beside Jason in the dirt of the flowerbed. "I knew that I must remain calm so he would be calm and not move," she said. "For all we knew at that time, Jason could have had several broken bones and internal injuries."

After six hours of tests and several x-rays, Lauren and Patrick were given the astonishingly good news that, outside of some sore muscles and a couple of superficial bruises, Jason was uninjured.

Later that evening, after things had settled down and Jason had gone to sleep, Patrick told Lauren exactly what he had witnessed as their son was falling. He was aware that Jason was falling in a north-south direction, which meant that his head would slam into the asphalt parking lot below.

Although a fall on such a hard surface might mean his son's death, Patrick was silent, mesmerized by the sight of Jason's entire body enveloped in a cloud.

As Patrick watched in awe, he beheld his smiling son slowly drifting downward. As he leaned forward on the windowsill to see more clearly, Patrick saw that nothing below him was visible. He could see no parking lot, no apartment building, no flowerbed— everything below Jason on his cloud was pure white.

By the time Patrick had sprinted down the stairs, he saw that the cloud bearing Jason had miraculously turned in an east-west direction, thereby moving away from the asphalt parking lot. Jason landed in the flowerbed of soft dirt and bark that cushioned his fall and saved his life.

Lauren said that Patrick had been reluctant to tell her about the angelic cloud that had enveloped their son and carried him safely to the soft earth and mulch of the flowerbed. "Patrick was in no way religious or spiritual," Lauren said. "He knew that I believed in life after death and in receiving divine assistance from angels when the need arose. He was simply awestruck by what he was seeing happening to save our son. That was why he told of Jason's accident in such a quiet and calm voice. He couldn't believe that he was actually witnessing a miracle and powerful proof that angels do exist and that they can intercede when we really need them."

*I*n 1995, when she and her husband moved into a large home with plenty of room for their four children to grow, Renay placed a plaque of a guardian angel on the wall in the hallway that led to the childrens' bedrooms.

"In fact," she said, "it was the very same angel plaque that my mother had placed in our home when I was young. I told my children the story of the guardian angel and the importance of the plaque to me. When I was around six or seven, I had suffered from terrible nightmares, and I was afraid of every shadow in my room. Mom got the plaque and hung it on a wall in the hallway outside of my bedroom. She said that this special guardian angel would keep all the bad dreams away from me and always protect our house and everyone in it from evil. My bad dreams seemed to stop after she got the angel plaque, and I cherished the object throughout my childhood.

Shortly before my mother passed away, she gave the angel to me."

Renay followed her mother's tradition and placed the plaque on the upstairs hallway wall, where it could keep watch over each of the children in their respective rooms, whether asleep or at play.

On the coldest day of the year in January 1996, Renay's family suffered a devastating house fire.

"It was started by our four-year-old daughter, who was playing with a discarded 'child-proof' lighter in her bedroom," Renay wrote. "I was on the phone when the smoke detector sounded. I was not thinking of the possibility of an actual fire raging upstairs, because we had had problems with the detector sounding without reason for three days prior."

As Renay approached the stairway, she was shocked to see smoke and flames. There really was a fire, a terrible blaze sweeping through the upstairs of their home.

The three older children were watching television in the family room downstairs. Renay clasped the hands of the two younger children and told the oldest to start running for the outside door. She knew it was freezing cold outside, and she grabbed their coats off the pegs by the door as they rushed past it.

"I was running out of the door with the three kids just as my husband was coming home from work," she said. "But I didn't have my baby!"

With a commingled expression of horror and grief twisting his features, Renay's husband emitted a cry for God's help and guidance as he ran up the stairs and into the room where the fire raged.

"There he saw our daughter, still sitting on the floor cross-legged, staring at the flames that swelled around her," Renay said. "Our baby was not touched by the flames, heat, or even smoke. She was safe!"

The next day, Renay's father, oldest brother, and she walked through what remained of the well-built older home that had once served their family so comfortably. As they carefully walked up the ice-covered steps to the second floor, Renay caught sight of the guardian-angel plaque on the wall.

"It was not burned, but covered with soot," Renay said. "Everything around it was either melted or burned, but the plaque remained."

Renay took the plaque in her hands and held it in front of her as she wept. "Thank you for protecting my baby," she said softly, looking at the plaque, her tears falling directly onto the completely blackened family heirloom.

And then, Renay said, almost instantaneously, a life-sized image of the guardian angel on the plaque began to appear through the blackness, right before their eyes.

"We all saw it," Renay testified. "After the image of the angel had faded back into the blackness, we all agreed that the angel had the exact likeness of the one on the plaque of the guardian angel that Mom had bought for our home so many years ago.

"Through the fire, the guardian angel protected not only my children, but also the beloved plaque she adorns," Renay said, concluding her story. "I still have the plaque. It remains blackened, and some of the varnish has chipped off, but she still watches over my family, as she will watch over the families of my children for many years to come."

*J*ack vividly recalls the late afternoon in July 2005 when he gathered around his grandfather's hospital bed with his father, Ryan, his two uncles, Miles and Devin, and four of his cousins. Grandpa Brendan was dying and members of the immediate family had been summoned to his bedside by the head nurse on the floor.

"I was eighteen and had just graduated from high school," Jack said. "My dad, Ryan, was the oldest of the men in his family. His two brothers were quite a bit younger, and they and everyone else looked to Dad in times like these. Of course, we hadn't really had a time like this since Grandma had died four years ago."

Jack remembered how difficult it was to see his grandfather lying in the hospital bed, gasping for air from the oxygen tube in his nostrils.

"Grandpa had been a longshoreman in New York before he married Grandma and moved to Rhode

11

Island and bought a little mom-and-pop store in the neighborhood where my dad and uncles had grown up," Jack said. "I can remember how strong my dad always said that Grandpa had been. Just a year ago, when Grandpa got sick at age eighty-six, Dad had said that he would shake it. Dad told all of us in the family that Grandpa was a tough old bird."

And now, the family faced the grim reality that Jack's father had been wrong in his optimistic diagnosis. Grandpa was dying in spite of his oldest son's assurances of his invulnerability.

The window to the room was open, and Jack could hear the laughter of children playing in a nearby park. It seemed somehow very wrong to him that while his family was solemnly gathered around a hospital bed, awaiting his beloved grandfather's final moments, that the rest of the world could be happy, playing, laughing, completely unaware that a once strong and proud man was struggling to hold on to his last gasps of life and breath. It seemed to Jack that the world should be mourning Grandpa Brendan.

Grandpa said something in a hoarse whisper, and Ryan leaned forward to listen and to ask him to repeat what he had said.

"I have never seen Dad look as desperate and at a loss as he did when he stood up and turned to face the rest of us," Jack said. "In a whisper not much louder than Grandpa's, Dad said that Grandpa wanted us to pray the Rosary."

Jack said that they all stood shifting uncomfortably, looking at each other hopefully, then looking away, feeling the strain of guilt and more than a small touch of helplessness and religious awkwardness: None of them knew the words of the Rosary.

Grandpa Brendan had been reared a strict Roman Catholic. He had attended church with his parents until he left to go out on his own. He often told his family that he had even been an altar boy.

When Grandpa fell in love with Grandma, who was a lapsed Catholic, he still regularly attended Mass and went to confession. After they were married and moved to Rhode Island, he remained a faithful churchgoer. After the children came and the young couple were working long hours seven days a week, church attendance began to become very expendable. By the time the three children had reached school age, the family's church attendance included only Christmas and Easter. When the boys went off on their own, got jobs, and got married, none of them attended church at all.

"We couldn't say that we were 'fallen away Catholics,'" Jack said, "because we had never been Catholics at all. But now a man that we had all loved, respected, and admired was begging us to pray the Rosary around his deathbed."

Jack's cousin, Nicole, who was in eighth grade, said that she had heard a friend of hers praying the Rosary. "I think it starts out, 'O Mary, you are the mother of Jesus, born in Bethlehem,' but I don't remember the rest," she said.

Grandfather began to weep, saying that it meant so much to him that they would pray the Rosary for him around his bed.

"Grandpa's tears and his crying made us all feel terrible," Jack said. "Dad said that he would send for a priest, but Grandpa said that he wanted the family to pray the Rosary as they stood in a circle around his bed."

Uncle Miles said that since Ryan was the oldest son, he must remember hearing their father pray the Rosary.

"Dad gave it a try," Jack said. "We gathered around Grandpa's bed, joined hands, and Dad told us to repeat the words after he said them. He more or less started out like Nicole had, then the prayer soon deteriorated into a meaningless jumble of words as we tried to follow his lead. Poor Grandpa became so stressed that he began to cry in deep sobs of despair."

Jack said that just as the family was feeling about as low as they possibly could, a Roman Catholic nun entered the room and asked if she might be of service. She told them that she had been passing in the hall and had heard them stumbling over the words of the Rosary.

"To my eyes, she was the quintessential Roman Catholic Sister," Jack said. "She wore the traditional black habit, and she carried a large crucifix in addition to a Rosary. She was quite tall and carried herself in a way that was almost rigid and somewhat restrained. All in all, she was quite an imposing figure, but her smile was so kind and her blue eyes seemed to be able to look right into a person's mind and tell what he was thinking."

Jack's father thanked her and asked her to please lead them in the praying of the Rosary.

The nun knelt at Grandpa's bedside and prayed the Lord's Prayer. Then, in a voice that touched each of the family members with a warmth and reverence, she began: "Hail Mary, full of grace, the Lord is with you. Blessed are you among women, and blessed is the fruit of your womb, Jesus. Holy Mary, Mother of God, pray for us sinners now and in the hour of our death."

After about the third time the Sister had repeated the prayer, most of them were able to pray the words along with her, and they were pleased to see a smile on the lips of Grandpa Brendan. Jack knows that each member of the family allowed their tears to flow unchecked.

Jack thought that the nun had led them in prayer nine or ten times before she rose and made the sign of the cross over Grandpa Brendan. She smiled and gave a blessing to each of the family members. Jack said that he would always remember her beautiful smile and the sound of her voice.

Grandfather passed away the next afternoon. He was a man who had lived a full and rich life, and he had many friends in the old neighborhood and throughout the city. The large number of persons attending the funeral gave testimony that Grandfather Brendan had been beloved by many.

A few days after the burial service, Jack's father told the family that he wished to thank the nun personally for her kindness.

Jack said that he accompanied his father to the hospital that afternoon. "When we inquired at the nurses' desk about who from the convent served that floor and ministered to the sick and the dying, the head nurse told us that they had no Roman Catholic sister who visited their floor on any regular basis," he said. "Dad explained that this nun had been in the hall and had overheard us trying to pray the Rosary. She had entered Grandpa's room and had been very kind to the family."

The nurse said that it must have been a nun who had been visiting another patient or a member of her own family, because they had no nun to attend patients at that hospital. She added that she was on duty that night when the family had gathered in Grandpa's room and she could say with certainty that there had been no nun on the floor that night that she had seen.

Puzzled, but assuming that the nurse's memory was incorrect, Jack and his father went to the telephone directory and found that there was a convent on the edge of the city. They knew that a kind and compassionate sister had come to their spiritual aid that night, and they would not give up their quest to thank the woman.

They drove directly to the convent and requested to see the Mother Superior.

"The first thing that struck us," Jack said, "was how informally the women were dressed at the convent. We didn't see anyone dressed in what we thought was the traditional habit that all sisters wore. They even let their hair show."

Jack and his father didn't have long to wait before an attractive middle-aged woman approached them and introduced herself as the Mother Superior. She, too, was dressed simply, and the clerical collar she wore was the only real hint that she was from a religious order.

"We definitely were not visiting the convent in *The Sound of Music*," Jack said. "Dad told the Mother Superior why we were there, and he described the nun who had been so kind and gracious to us in our hour of need. Dad said that we really wanted to thank her for her compassion in helping Grandpa pass peacefully."

The Mother Superior listened to their description of the tall, almost regal nun, and she smiled when

Jack and his father described her black and white traditional habit. She explained that their order had not
worn such "uniforms" since the 1970s. She asked them
to look around at the sisters present in the convent.

"Dad insisted that our wonderful nun had been
wearing the kind of habit that he remembered as a
young boy when he had attended church services
with his father," Jack said. "The Mother Superior
only smiled and suggested once again that we look
around and see for ourselves if we found any such
nuns residing in the convent."

When Jack and his father left the convent, they
sat quietly in their car for several minutes before
either of them spoke.

"We know what we saw," his father said. "We
know that someone appeared in answer to our
spiritual need and came to comfort us and to give
Grandpa peace of mind and spirit. We know we
aren't crazy. We saw her. Who or what did we see?"

Jack said he chose his words carefully before he
answered. "Dad, either we were visited by the spirit,
the ghost, of a compassionate nun who came in
response to our need, or we were blessed by an angel
from a higher realm. We can take our pick, but I am
going to go with the angel."

$\mathcal{B}$ ack in the 1970s, when he was only seven years old, Brody became very aware that he had a guardian angel.

"Our house consisted of three levels," he explained, "a basement, a main floor with three bedrooms, and an upstairs with two bedrooms. When they had first moved in, Mom and Dad slept in the master bedroom and Bobby, my younger brother, and I each had our own rooms. We didn't really use the upstairs."

When Brody's mom became pregnant, his parents decided that he would move to an upstairs bedroom and his room on the main floor would be converted into the nursery for the new arrival.

Brody emphasized that in no way did he resent the move to an upstairs bedroom; he was eager and excited to change bedrooms and the move wasn't being forced upon him in any way. He said his parents were always very loving toward him and his brother.

Shortly after he had moved upstairs, Brody was playing with his five-year-old brother on the main floor. They had been chasing each other around the dining room, when Brody decided to quit the game of tag and go upstairs to his room.

As he began to walk up the steps, he was startled to see a lady in white standing at the top of the stairs.

"She was wearing a dress that had a strange banner across it," Brady said. "As weird as it sounds, it looked the kind of banner that Miss America would wear."

Brady recalled that he quickly turned around and went back down the steps. That night, he slept in his brother's room.

"I told my parents what I had seen," Brady said, "but they were understanding and didn't give me a lecture about seeing things or watching too much spooky television programs."

Brady's next encounter with the Lady in White occurred one evening when his parents were out and Bobby and he were at home with a babysitter.

"I was upstairs, sitting on the floor of my room, watching my little television set when I felt something brush against me," Brady said. "Thinking it was Bobby sneaking up on me, I turned around quickly—and there stood the Lady in White."

That was when Brady heard a gentle, soothing feminine voice tell him not to be afraid. "I know you, Brady," she said. "I know you, and I love you. I know you, and I love you."

Brady listened to the Lady in White saying those words over and over. Then he managed to get to his feet and make his way downstairs.

He did not tell the babysitter about the mysterious woman in white who had visited him in his room upstairs. Brady slept with Bobby again that night.

When he told his mom the next day, she said that either Brady was dreaming about his guardian angel or his angel was paying him a visit.

Brady saw the Lady in White in his room twice more, but on neither occasion did she speak. She only smiled and made him aware of her presence.

While some people might judge Brady's Lady in White to be the product of an overactive or very creative seven-year-old mind, he feels that he has strong testimony in support of his theory that he did, indeed, receive visits from his guardian angel.

Two years later, when Brady was in the fourth grade, his parents were visiting his classroom during a parent-teacher conference. At one point in the discussion about her son, Brady's mother felt prompted to tell his teacher about the Lady in White.

"My teacher immediately told my mother not to say any more about the Lady until she returned, saying that she would be right back," Brady said. "When she returned, she brought my second-grade teacher, who still taught at the school and who was also there that evening for parent-teacher conferences.

"I had never spoken a word about the Lady in White to any of my teachers—or to anyone outside of my family," Brady stressed. "My second-grade teacher then told my parents that on more than one occasion while I was in her class, she had seen the apparition of a lady dressed in white in the back of the classroom. And something she said she would never forget: the apparition appeared to be wearing some kind of banner."

The teacher had kept her own counsel about the apparition and had only recently confided about the strange experience to some of the other teachers, one of whom was his fourth-grade teacher.

"That was why, as soon as Mom started talking about my Lady in White, my fourth-grade teacher had excused herself from their conference to get my second-grade teacher," Brady said. "When she heard about my guardian angel, she was relieved. She had not been going crazy."

Brady said that neither he nor anyone else sighted the Lady in White after the appearances witnessed by his second-grade teacher. Perhaps, one might theorize the benevolent entity only wished for another to witness her presence.

*J*essica, a fifty-year-old artist, was traveling on a Mississippi highway when her pickup truck was hit from behind. Her body crashed through the windshield, struck a roadside sign, then landed hard on the sun-baked pavement. In the process, she broke both legs, shattered her pelvis and right hip, and compressed three of her vertebrae.

It was during the time that her body was airborne that she knew she died. Jessica felt her body rise and move through a spinning tunnel. She felt nothing, but she heard the last of her breath leave her body as it struck the pavement.

As she moved through the tunnel, she could see a door from which bright light issued, and she could also hear the sound of choral music. Then she saw something so incredibly bright that it took her a moment to recognize the same angel that had pulled her from a swimming pool when she was eight and that had stood at her bedside at age twelve when she underwent an emergency appendectomy.

Jessica said the angel always appears with no wings or halo, and with a hood that covers its head. The glow that surrounds the being's form is so bright that she has never been able to distinguish the eyes or mouth of the angel, but she can make out the hands and arms. The brilliant illumination that seems to emanate from the angelic spirit guide itself is comprised of a white light with flecks of blue and yellow.

And always, Jessica said, the angelic being's voice was very calm, distinct, soothing, and assuring. Upon hearing its words of comfort, she felt surrounded by love and all fear left her.

The angel pointed to its left, and Jessica looked down to perceive her own lifeless body. She was lying on her back, and there was blood all around her.

It was at that point in the experience that the angel asked her if she were ready to leave the world. No, she answered. She had a husband and two small kids. She had too much to do; she had to go back.

The angelic light being nodded its head, and Jessica was next aware of everything going black.

But the darkness lasted for only a brief period of time, and when she looked up, she saw her husband and a number of medical personnel. Her request had been granted—she was alive.

Jessica spent the next fifty-eight days in the hospital. The light being visited her four more times while her shattered body was mending.

Jessica acknowledged that things had looked pretty grim for a time, but her guardian angel told her not to worry.

She spent five months in a wheelchair, and the doctors told Jessica that she would never walk again.

"But now I can walk with a cane," Jessica said. "My recovery was a miracle, but then, I believe in miracles."

Because of the miraculous blessing of her dramatic recovery, the focus of Jessica's art is now based on her lifelong experiences with the brilliant angels of light. Many have found inspiration and hope in her vivid and colorful scenes of angelic encounters.

After one of our lectures, Caleb told us that he had attended a kind of angelic night school since he was a young boy and that he has continued to remain in contact with his celestial tutors throughout his adult life.

"At first, two angels would come to me and lift me from my physical body as I lay in bed, but soon I was able to slip out of the body without their assistance," Caleb said. "As soon as I was out of the body, I would receive instruction from angelic teachers. I suppose you could say it was like going to night school. During the day, I went to junior high. At night, my soul body was taken up to a higher plane to attend an angel school."

One of the lessons that the angels taught Caleb was how to heal himself and others.

When he was sixteen, he was scheduled for surgery because he had taken an elbow to the eye during basketball practice and it had become badly infected. Caleb said that he had ignored the pain and blurred vision and didn't realize how serious the infection had become until their family doctor was calling the hospital to make arrangements for surgery the next morning.

"I began to use the healing methods that my angels had taught me," Caleb said, "and I asked for some angelic assistance. The next morning, my astonished mother took me to the hospital for the surgeon to verify that the infection had vanished overnight and that my eye was completely healed."

Caleb continued to use his healing abilities throughout junior high and secondary school. Nothing too dramatic like healing his eye, he said, just minor things, like fixing a teammate's sprain or dislocated shoulder. On one occasion, however, he placed his hands on the chest of an older teacher who was having a heart attack and reversed the episode. Doctors credited Caleb's resourceful use of "massage" with saving the man's life.

"I am often asked if such double schooling wasn't tiring," Caleb said. "On the contrary, I used to awaken in the morning feeling completely refreshed. Now that I am in my forties, I have developed my level of awareness so that I am aware of my guides' presence without leaving the physical body and I have quietly used my healing gifts to help many family members, friends, and fellow employees in my office."

*J*ohn is a field service engineer for a large
company that specializes in electronic security. Twenty-some years ago, the company for which
he worked required that the employees use their own
vehicles to perform field service work. John had a
pickup that he employed in this capacity. He recalled
that there was no camper shell on it, and it was a
rather plain, bronze-colored four-wheel drive truck.

In those days, the drive from San Jose along
U.S. 101 down to Lockwood passed through mostly
farmland. John recalled that it was about a two and
one-half hour drive.

On this particular day, John had stopped at a
roadside sandwich stand and bought a couple of hot
dogs and a couple of cans of soda for the drive. As he
turned out of the dirt lot to head back to the freeway
on-ramp, he looked both ways and saw no one. Not

a single soul.

"When I pulled onto the road, there was this guy standing at the freeway on-ramp," John said. "There were no trees, signs, or bushes that he could have been hidden behind. No other vehicles had passed that could have dropped him there.

"As I drew near," John continued, "I could see that he was dressed as a contemporary cowboy. Jeans, chambray shirt, boots—but minus the Western-style hat. As for his age, he seemed to be in that period of this life where he could have been anywhere from fifty to mid-sixties. He was at least six feet tall, clean shaven, with dark hair that was more than halfway to silver, and with that kind of tan that comes from a lifetime spent outdoors. He was what my wife refers to as 'ruggedly handsome.' He carried a single, rather battered, leather satchel. I think my father used to call them 'AWOL bags' from the time he was in the Army."

The hitchhiker put his thumb out, and John thought, "What the heck; it'll be nice to have someone to talk to on the drive."

When John asked where the stranger was headed, he answered Jolon, a small town just north of Lockwood. John told him that he was in luck—he was headed to Lockwood—and to hop in.

The hitchhiker eyed the two hot dogs on the center of the bench seat and asked if John was planning for company.

John laughed and told him, "No, but you're welcome to have one, and a soda, too."

He asked what John had put on them, and John replied that he had only smeared some brown mustard on the hot dogs. The hitcher beamed, picked one up, and said, "Just how I like 'em!"

John admitted that he was used to wolfing down his food, especially when he was driving. "This guy was so dainty as he ate that hot dog," John recalled. "It was clear that he was savoring every bite. As we rolled through Gilroy, about ten minutes into the drive, I asked him how the dog was. He bobbed his head, and said he hadn't had a hot dog in a very long time, and it was nice to have one this good."

John remembers that there were things about the stranger that were just a wee bit off. "Some of his physical mannerisms, some of his speech, his choice of words; but I had grown up in an Army family, moved around a lot, and met all kinds of different people. Everyone is a little off, so I didn't think too much of it."

The two men talked "about this and that" on the drive. John learned that the hitcher's name was Willie and that he was going to see about a position as a foreman on a ranch near Jolon.

"His languid drawl as he spoke placed me curiously at ease," John said. "I, in turn, told him my name and that I had just started this job not quite a year ago. I told him that I enjoyed it very much, and that I could see spending my life happily at this job. He thought that rather odd for someone who was only twenty-two at the time. He wanted to know why I didn't have more of a yearning to see more of the world."

John told him of growing up Army and having seen more of the world than he cared to. Willie eyed him speculatively and just nodded sagely.

As they drove down Jolon Road headed toward town, Willie announced that they were nearing his stop. He directed John to pull off to the side of the road near a gate. John shut off the truck and sat with this stranger in the early afternoon sun.

Willie was preparing to dismount, but he stopped and opened his satchel. He pulled out a huge silver belt buckle, bigger than a large butter dish. John could see that the buckle was obviously handmade and that it had to weigh probably ten to twelve ounces.

"In the center of the buckle was one of the biggest pieces of turquoise that I had ever seen on a piece of jewelry," John said. "I love turquoise. Especially that from the Sleeping Beauty Mine. It has a rich, incomparable blue color that just resonates with me. This stone just was absolutely perfect. Outstanding. I was nearly certain it came from that mine because of its color."

Willie asked John if he wanted to buy it. John told him that there was no way that he could afford something as magnificent as that buckle.

"Sure you can," Willie smiled. "I'll trade you for however much you have in your wallet."

In John's wallet was $53. That buckle was worth much more than that, and he told Willie so.

But Willie shrugged and said, "That's fine. I'll take the fifty-three dollars, and we'll call it square."

"I can't do that to you," John protested. "We both know that buckle is worth between three hundred and four hundred dollars."

Willie shrugged.

"Why do you want to sell it for so little?" John asked.

"I need the money," Willie answered simply.

"For?" John was looking at Willie intently, trying to figure out the strange man.

"If I don't get the job, I'll need bus fare home and hopefully something to eat along the way," Willie offered as an explanation for his willingness to sell such a valuable object for so little money.

John reached into his wallet and pulled out the $53. "Here," he said. "Take it, and keep your buckle."

"Now that wouldn't be fair, son!" Willie exclaimed.

John had a ready response. "It wouldn't be fair if I accepted your buckle in trade. You and I both know it would be the same as if I had stolen it from you."

Willie appeared uncomfortable with John's unselfish generosity to a stranger. "How am I supposed to square this if you won't accept it?" he asked.

John frowned his puzzlement, not entirely sure of Willie's meaning.

Willie sighed, somewhat impatiently. "I mean, how am I to repay this debt? You place me in your debt."

John had an easy solution to Willie's dilemma: If he should ever come upon someone who needed a little help, he should remember that someone had helped him once, and if he could, he should offer to help. That would be more than adequate payment.

Then John added, "Fifty-three dollars is fifty-three dollars, but I'm young and healthy and I can earn it again."

Willie stared at him for what seemed a very long time until John began to feel rather uncomfortable. "You're much older than twenty-two, boy," Willie said, finally breaking his silence.

Willie accepted the proffered money with thanks and got out of John's truck. Once he was on the road, he leaned through the open window and offered his hand.

When John took the hitchhiker's hand, he was amazed at the man's strength. "I don't think I could have broken that grip had I tried," John said. "He didn't crush my hand, he just locked it in place. I've never run across anyone with a grip like that."

Willie stared in John's eyes and said, "It is a rare thing to meet someone not driven by avarice and sheer greed. I don't think you have anything to worry about. I think you'll do just fine at your job."

Willie now spoke precisely and enunciated each word in a manner not consistent with their earlier conversation.

"It was almost as if it was a proclamation," John said, recalling the impact of those words. "The manner in which he spoke made me uneasy for a reason I cannot articulate. It was just a feeling gnawing at the back of my brain."

John smiled at him and stumbled over his thanks. Willie released John's hand and withdrew from the truck.

"He stooped to pick up his bag, and I turned my attention to starting the truck," John said. "I looked up to wave to Willie and make sure he was clear of the truck—and he was nowhere to be seen.

"Where I had stopped, I could see up the road ahead of me and down the road behind me. I could

see across the road into a vacant pasture and over to
the field behind the gate. I didn't see him."

Fearing that maybe Willie had fallen beside the
truck, John turned off the engine and got out. He
raced around to the passenger's side and saw nothing. He looked in the bed: Empty except for his hand
truck, tools, and equipment cases.

"The hair was starting to stand up on the back of
my neck," John said. "I backed away from the truck,
slowly sank down, and looked under it. Nothing.
I stood up and looked around. There was nowhere for
this guy to have gotten to in roughly thirty seconds.
No trees to hide behind. No bushes. No ditches.
Nothing.

"Immediately, the story about that hitchhiking
girl that would disappear from a car after giving
directions popped into my head, and I felt a little
sick.

"I called his name a few times, and the only
response I got was the wind rattling through the dry
grass. I got back in my truck and took a deep breath
and got the hell out of there."

John said that all through the job in Lockwood,
his wallet burned in his right hip pocket.

"I couldn't pull it out and look inside to see if
perhaps the money was still there, and I had imagined the whole episode," John said. "I was just too

fearful. I've never used drugs in my life, so if somehow the money was still in my wallet, I struggled with the awful thought of how I would account for the incident. Wild scenarios raced through my brain as I worked the afternoon away."

Upon finishing the job, John had his invoice signed and walked back to his truck parked in the now nearly empty lot. He put his tools in the bed of the truck, and finally found enough strength to pull out his wallet.

John confided that the most frightened he had ever been was the time some hunters had mistaken him for a deer and had opened fire on him as he ran through the hills in the early morning. Opening that wallet, he said, was on par with getting shot at.

It was empty.

John had given all his money to a strange, vanishing hitchhiker named Willie. There was no other explanation.

After hearing us discuss visitations by mysterious beings on a national radio program, John began to think about the twenty years that had passed since he encountered Willie.

John has survived three layoffs on three different occasions by three different management teams when the company was restructured. People more senior than John lost their jobs, but John was never let go.

John remained with the company even after it was bought by a huge multinational conglomerate. Immediately after acquiring the company, management cut nearly 30 percent of the workforce. Once again, employees with more seniority than John lost their jobs.

There have been two additional layoffs by this conglomerate as they reorganized segments within the business unit of which John is a part. Yet again, people with more seniority than he lost their jobs.

When the conglomerate combined districts just a year ago, it was the same remarkable story. Dozens of people lost their jobs, but John stayed. Over the years, John said, several people with whom he had worked closely committed suicide while employed at the company.

"I'm still here," John said. "I'm still happily doing a job that I love."

Did the mysterious hitchhiker bless John? Was Willie an angel in disguise?

John is beginning to conclude that that was the case.

"I don't want to think what would have happened if I had accepted that belt buckle," he said.

When she was seven years old, an angel pulled Addison out of the path of an automobile. She remembers vividly this beautiful being of light that grabbed her by the neck of her sweater and pulled her back to the front yard of her home.

The friends with whom she had been playing were left openmouthed and awestruck. Alerted by the children's screams, Addison's mother came running from their backyard where she had been raking leaves. Clutching Addison in her arms, she heard the children tell how her daughter had chased the ball into the street and forgot to stop, look, and listen, and how she had almost been hit by a car, but then went up in the air and flew backward onto the soft grass and leaves of the yard.

Addison remembers laughing and crying at the same time. "I wanted to jump up and down and tell everyone about the beautiful angel that I could see standing right beside us. I could not take my eyes off of him. He was simply magnificent."

Before the angel took leave of the scene, he told Addison that he would always be near, watching over her, and that she should always remember to pray every day.

Word spread at school about Addison's incredible escape, and classmates continued to ask her how she had managed to fly like that.

Addison tried to explain that it was an angel that had lifted her into the air and pulled her back to safety. Some of her friends believed her; others teased her for believing in angels. There were certain kids who were obviously uncomfortable with any religious or "weird" talk that tried to make her seem as though she was more holy or special than the rest of them.

Pretty soon, Addison herself began to make jokes about her marvelous feats of levitation in an attempt to put a stop to the ridiculous local urban legends growing up around her miraculous rescue. The Sally Field television series *The Flying Nun* was popular at the time, and for years afterward, Addison was nicknamed "the Flying Nut" by kids at school.

For many years, Addison had heeded her guardian angel's admonition to pray every day. She would kneel beside her bed at night and ask for protection from evil while she slept. Upon rising in the morning, she would thank God for a new day and ask that her angel look after her. And, of course, she always prayed earnestly before a math test or a big basketball game.

And now, thirty-five years later, in August 2002, the forty-two-year-old Addison was lying on a hospital gurney, the victim of a hit-and-run, about to be wheeled in for emergency surgery.

"I was in and out of consciousness," Addison said, "and I remember wondering if it was the same car that had missed me when I was seven coming back for another crack at me. I also wondered where my guardian angel was this time. Maybe you only got one chance to be rescued."

Then, Addison said, she felt someone take her hand. Turning her head, expecting to see her husband walking at the side of the gurney, Addison saw the same beautiful angelic figure beside her. In answer to her unspoken question, the angel said that some things could not be changed. He was sorry that she had been injured, but he would be there to be certain that she healed well and quickly.

When she regained consciousness in the recovery room, Addison's husband and two children were at her side. All three of them were crying, and for a moment, Addison feared the worst.

"In reality," Addison said, "they were crying because the surgeon had informed them that the damage done to my body was not as severe as they had at first assessed. In fact, outside of a few broken ribs, a lot of bruises, and a pretty badly busted-up right leg, it was truly miraculous that I had not sustained more injuries."

Addison joined her family in their tears of happiness and smiled in the awareness that her angel had interceded once again on her behalf. She had remained conscious enough in the ambulance on the way to the hospital to overhear the EMTs saying that she had been struck as she crossed with the light, and that she had been thrown many feet into the center of the intersection. It seemed terrifyingly obvious to Addison from the medics' remarks that she might be fatally injured.

Throughout Addison's two-week stay in the hospital, she had a number of visits from her guardian angel. She doesn't know if these were in the dream state, but the late-night sessions seemed to her to be in the nature of visions. Sometime during each experience, the angel passed his hands over Addison's body in what she understood and felt to be healing ministrations.

On one occasion, Addison said that they engaged in a dialogue that she feels was intended to be shared with others.

"The beautiful Light Being said that he wished to speak to me of spirituality," Addison said. "He told me that in terms of collective humanity, humans remained in a very primitive state. He reminded me that when he saved me from the path of the automobile when I was seven, that he had instructed me to pray."

Addison told her guardian that she had heeded him and had always prayed each evening and morning, and that she had taught her children to follow her example.

The guardian angel sighed and told her that her concept of God remained primitive. In spite of the revelation and blessing that she had received as a child, she really didn't know how to pray.

"What you call prayer is more like poems of woe or the offering of excuses for your actions," he said. "You beseech God not to punish you for your misdeeds, or you beg to be forgiven for actions which you have every intention of repeating."

The brilliantly glowing entity said that begging for forgiveness was something that humans did only to assuage their personal feelings of guilt or shame. "It would be far better simply to live your lives in such a way that you will not feel the need to be asking forgiveness.

"When you pray," the being told Addison, "pray with joy. Prayer is a love song, and you have forgotten how to sing it."

After Addison returned to her home and her life, she said that she always resolved to make her prayers a love song to God and the benevolent universe. She has also made it her mission to share the words of her guardian angel with others.

*R*ick has no problem admitting that he got into trouble in the great northern woods because he was a smart-aleck kid from the big city who did not truly respect the wilderness. He also has no difficulty testifying to a visit from an angelic being that saved his life.

"Who gets lost in the woods in 1998?" Rick asked rhetorically. "A wise guy from Milwaukee who thinks he doesn't have to pay attention to the unyielding laws of nature and the lifelong experience of his grandparents in the forests of northern Wisconsin, that's who. I guess I deserved the term 'wisenheimer' that my grandma called me when I was a little kid of eight or nine. Well, I was twenty years old that fall and just as overconfident."

Rick was taking a course in photography at the university, and he decided to take a weekend drive up to his grandparents' cabin to take photos of the autumn leaves. Where could he find a place more vibrant and colorful than northern Wisconsin in October?

"I knew that Grandpa and Grandma had only recently moved back to their home in Stevens Point for the winter months, but I had a key to the place if I should decide to stay overnight in the cabin," Rick said. "Since I didn't get up there until around four o'clock in the afternoon, I was thinking that I could build a nice fire in the fireplace, relax, get a good night's sleep, and get an earlier start in the morning."

Rick remembered a very picturesque creek and small pond that was about a mile or so from the cabin. At twilight, it was bound to be teeming with deer and other wildlife. He would be able to get some fantastic pictures.

Rick set out on the old worn trail that went by the creek, but it was growing dark and he thought that he remembered a shortcut through the densely forested area that he had discovered during a summer's visit when he was thirteen or fourteen.

"The brush was a lot thicker than I remembered it," Rick said. "I was carrying my camera equipment and it became very difficult to walk without slipping in the heavy fall of leaves. There had apparently been a recent, rather heavy rainfall and walking on the wet leaves was like trying to walk on ice. I decided that I better get back on the familiar trail."

Darkness seemed to come on as quickly as if someone had turned off a light switch. Rick had not thought to bring a flashlight, and he often found himself walking into a tree or a low-hanging branch.

"When I realized that I was lost, I was almost paralyzed with fear," Rick said. "All the old warnings from my grandparents and old-timers in the area about wolves and bears came cascading down on me. Every chipmunk scampering in the leaves behind me became the paws of a grizzly bear thundering toward me, intent on swallowing me whole. If a bear didn't grab me, I figured that a pack of wolves would soon be closing in on me."

Rick did have enough commonsense to realize that he could hurt himself wandering around in the woods after dark. He sat and leaned back against a tree.

"After fighting off feelings of total humiliation, I realized that if I was going to get out of the woods alive, I would have to admit that I was a screw up and call for help on my cell phone," he said. "I discounted the possibility of having my roommate come to rescue me. He was over three hours away, and besides, he was from Chicago and probably couldn't even find my grandparents' cabin in broad daylight. My grandparents were also about three hours away in another direction. Grandpa was a master woodsman, but how could I explain to him where I was? It would have to be 911."

That was when Rick discovered that he was in an area where he could get no signal; his cell phone was useless.

Rick tried his best to smother the panic that was beginning to overtake him. He had no flashlight; he didn't smoke, so he had no matches or lighter with which to start a fire; he had no food or blankets; he had not even put on a heavy coat—he wore only a light-weight leather jacket. It was getting very cold, and it would get much colder before morning and light.

Rick closed his eyes, folded his hands, and began to pray as he had never before prayed in his life.

"This was not some Sunday school memorized job," he said. "This was a real from-the-depths-of-despair kind of prayer. This was a help-save-me kind of prayer."

After a few minutes, Rick opened his eyes because of the incredibly bright light that was shining through his eyelids. He thought the small tree off to his right was on fire, and he jumped to his feet.

Then he saw that the light was situated just in front of the tree, and that it was not fire at all.

A voice from the midst of the brilliant light called Rick's name and told him that he was his guardian angel, surrounded by God's light, from Heaven. It told him not to be afraid and to stay where he was. It said it would stay with him until help came.

"Somehow, I knew that the being speaking from within the light had always been with me and that he would always be around somewhere keeping an eye on me," Rick said. "I thought also of the story of Moses and the burning bush and the voice of the Angel of the Lord that spoke to him from the midst of the flames."

Feeling calm, peaceful, and protected, Rick fell asleep.

He was awakened by powerful flashlight beams slicing through the darkness toward him. Rick called out, and within a few minutes, half a dozen men were standing around him, asking if he was all right. His rescuers, who had been walking back to the cabin that they had rented for the weekend, said they had found him because of the bright fire he had started.

"They were really confused when they could not find a single trace of a campfire—no ashes, no soot, no burned spot, nothing," Rick said. "I had no way of explaining to them in rational terms that the brilliant light that had brought them to me was my guardian angel, so I just came out with it and called it the way I saw it. I think a couple of the men believed me, but the only thing that mattered to me was the glorious fact that I now had proof of what Sunday school teachers and preachers had been trying to tell me for years: Angels do exist, and sometimes, for whatever unfathomable reason, they decide to enter our world and save our skins."

helly always makes a point of reminding people that they should not place angels above God, but she firmly believes that angels are an unforgettable reminder that God truly cares about every detail of our lives.

Shelly is visually impaired. "I do have some sight," she explained, "but many factors affect it, such as the time of day, how bright the sun is, how much contrast is in the environment, and so on."

She recalled the "incredibly rainy day in midwinter" when she was out on the street. "Although it was only 3:30 P.M., it was getting dark," she said. "I fear dusk more than anything. I can see far better at night than when it is dusk."

Shelly was trying to get to a pharmacy where she would be able to turn in her utility bill. It was past due, and she really had to get it taken care of that day. Even though she had been to that pharmacy a hundred times, she became disoriented in the dusk and heavy rain.

"The manner in which the area was paved made it hard for me to distinguish between the sidewalk and the street," she said. "When I was nearly mowed down by a car, I stopped to pray. I was soaked to the skin, confused, and on the verge of tears."

Shelly declared that she is a quite independent person, but she realized that there was no getting herself out of this fix.

"Lord," she prayed. "I need your help. Please help me."

She wasn't even finished with the prayer when she heard a robust man's voice asking if he could help her.

"I looked up at him, and he appeared to be in his early sixties or late fifties," she said. "He was wearing a blue raincoat and a blue baseball cap. I think he had a patch on one shoulder. It looked like a post-man's uniform. He had a ruddy bronze complexion with a shock of white hair just above the roll of flesh on the back of his neck."

Shelly explained that she really hated to ask peo-ple for help, "Because people get carried away with the good deed of helping me until I'm overwhelmed. And they usually ask a lot of irrelevant questions about my condition."

She told the man that she was trying to get to the pharmacy and that she had to get there before they closed.

"Oh, I know where that is," he said in a cheerful voice.

"Here it comes!" Shelly thought. "Now I'll never get rid of him."

Then, according to Shelly, he did the most amazing thing. "He turned away from me and offered me his elbow. I about fell over. My own parents still try to push me ahead of them if they think I need guidance. Even my boyfriend didn't know how to guide me."

Shelly took his arm, and found that it was warm and surprisingly dry. As they walked, she became the one who started rattling away, about how she got herself into this predicament and that she had almost given up and thought she was going to have to sit somewhere until it got dark in order to find her way home.

"I needed to vent," she said. "I needed to just be heard without being told what to do or what I should have done or having to answer the question, 'How many fingers am I holding up?'"

The man never said another word; he just listened.

Shelly had a profound and growing sense that this man knew her very well. "He knew me better than anyone else I know," she said. "There was no doubt that he seemed to know everything about me."

When they rounded a particular corner, Shelly recognized where they were.

"Oh, thanks!" she told her benefactor. "I know where I am now."

But as she let go of his arm and turned to thank him, "There was no one there; no one. Just the rain. There were no footsteps walking away. Not even a shadow."

Shelly remembers that she seemed to stand on that corner in the rain "for the longest time, trying to comprehend what had just happened. It just couldn't be, but it was as real as everything else around me. When I thought about it, I hadn't heard any footsteps coming toward me when I was praying. I had been a little startled, in fact, because the nice person seemed to just appear out of nowhere."

Tears welled up in her eyes as she felt the reality of what had just occurred. For a moment, she feared the powerful emotions might pull her to the ground.

"Oh, God," she asked, turning her face up to meet the rain. "Do you think so much of me that you would send me an angel?"

Shelly thinks she's seen her angel possibly two other times. "I'm pretty certain about the second time," she said. "He was walking with a lady. I had a guide dog by this time, but I still, on occasion, got disoriented. He gave me the directions I asked for, then vanished."

In evaluating her supernatural experiences, Shelly thinks that God really wants people to be mostly unaware when they are interacting with an angel.

"God doesn't want us seeking after angels instead of Him," she said. "I don't think all angels are alike, and I definitely think they very often assume a very ordinary appearance in order to not draw attention away from what is more important.

"After all, it was not really about my meeting an angel. It was about God sending me exactly what His child needed. He just did it in a more tangible way than usual."

*H*er boss had just left to run a personal errand, leaving Angie alone to manage the ice cream and yogurt shop, when a man in his mid-twenties entered and sat down at the counter. Angie, a psychology major at a nearby university, often formed instant analyses of her customers and tried to imagine their life stories, but this guy was an easy call. He appeared nervous, ill at ease, and he kept glancing around the empty shop as if checking for any other employees who might be in the back. Angie made a preliminary analysis that she might be in for a bad time with this guy.

He ordered a dish of strawberry yogurt, joking that since he had arrived recently in California from back east, he was happy that the stores had strawberries all year round. Angie resisted informing him that the flavored ingredients in the yogurt could just as easily be available in New Jersey as the West Coast.

Angie was used to men trying weak jokes and clever remarks to flirt with her, but she became increasingly concerned that this customer was up to no good.

When he gave her a five-dollar bill to pay for the yogurt, there was a note attached informing her that he was robbing the shop and that she must hand over every cent in the cash register—or else. Angie didn't see a knife or a gun on the man, but she could clearly see the desperation in his eyes.

It was at the very moment that Angie read the scrawled demand and the emphatic threat that she suddenly felt a strange sense of calm throughout her body. At the same time, she heard a gentle, yet authoritative voice, instructing her to remain quiet and in control.

Later, Angie recalled that it was as if she were taking dictation from the voice. "It was more or less a feminine voice," she said, "and it told me to do as the man demanded and to talk pleasantly to him. Strangely enough, I did what the voice suggested, though my normal reaction would have been to try to get the heck out of there."

To show her compliance, Angie opened the cash drawer and gave him the money, less than $100. "It's been a slow day so far," she explained, as he quickly riffled through the bills. When he frowned at the small amount, Angie asked if he wanted the coins, as well.

He shook his head, then slumped forward on his elbows on the counter. Angie wished that he would leave now that he had the money, but the man just remained there, as if he really had no other place to go.

Then, prompted again by the soft, feminine voice that seemed now to be coming from over her right shoulder, Angie asked the holdup man why he was so troubled, so desperate that he would pull a robbery of a yogurt shop in broad daylight.

When he lifted his head to answer, he told her that he had just been released from jail to find a huge stack of bills awaiting him. He had spent the last ten days searching for work, but he was unable to find a job. His wife and two kids had left him to go live with her parents in another state and he missed them so much that he was going crazy.

To her astonishment, Angie found herself consoling the man, assuring him that he was important in God's eyes and that he shouldn't do anything that might put him back in jail. He needed to be strong, to know that there were angels looking out for him. The angelic beings would help him find a better path in life if only he would reach out for the Light of God and Goodness.

Angie and the holdup man sat talking for over an hour. When customers came into the shop, he allowed her to wait on them, giving her whatever change she needed when they paid for their yogurt or ice cream. Finally, he returned all but $10 to the cash drawer, pleading that he needed to keep a few bucks.

When customers left the shop, Angie would return to the holdup man to channel some more heavenly advice. Over and over, she reminded him that God would change his life if only he would permit Him to enter his heart.

After nearly two hours, the would-be thief left the shop with the promise that he would return sometime to speak with Angie. He told her that he would do his best to turn over a new leaf, to walk a pathway that would include God.

Shortly after the holdup man had gone, Angie's manager returned and she told him what had transpired in their shop in his absence. The manager agreed that the man's tale of woe was touching, and he expressed his approval of Angie's turning the money over to the robber rather than trying to resist. He was not at all concerned about losing $10, but he convinced Angie that she did not really know what the man might be capable of if he couldn't find work and became even more desperate for money.

Angie conceded that her manager had a valid point. The holdup man's next victims might not be so fortunate as to have an angel whisper in their ear. During the course of their conversation, the robber had told Angie his name and certain other particulars. Although she suffered from feelings of having betrayed a confidence, she told her manger to call the police.

Upon his arrest, the man stated that he held no bitterness toward Angie. He informed her attorney that he was glad that she had helped him find God and discover that there were people like Angie in the world who were willing to help him change his life.

"My car accident in 1999 was a wake-up call to follow a more spiritual path in life," Riley recalls.

After the impact of the crash, Riley felt she was floating outside of both the car and her physical body. An angel appeared and told her that she now had a choice to go or to stay.

The angel brought Riley close to her physical body to survey the damage.

"My chest had been crushed, and it was apparent that my heart had suffered damage," Riley recalled. "The angel showed me a projection of a kind of alternate reality. If I decided to live, I saw a scenario of myself in the hospital and healing. If I did not wish to undergo that reality, I could very easily let my spirit go."

Riley told her angel guardian that she must stay on Earth.

When she regained consciousness, she found herself in an ambulance, speeding to an emergency room at a hospital.

"I felt great pain," Riley said, "and I realized that I was back in my body and that I had the choice to stay. For a few hours, I must admit that I reconsidered my decision."

Miraculously, the crushing impact to her chest left Riley with less serious injuries than had at first been feared. Although several ribs had been broken, the ER doctors made the decision that surgery was not necessary. Riley was kept in the hospital for a few days for observation and allowed to recover without any invasive heart procedures.

Not only had the angel allowed Riley to make the decision whether or not to stay, in addition to cushioning what could have been a fatal blow to her chest, the celestial guardian had endowed her with a special gift.

Riley said that she now had the ability to communicate with every single cell and atom that made up her body. For the first time in her life, she could make contact with every nerve and blood vessel, and she was able to use this open line of communication to heal miraculously fast.

"Other than rest in the hospital," Riley said, "I never received any surgical procedures or any other treatment of any kind. All I needed was the time to allow my body to respond."

Riley admitted that she still feels some pain from the accident, but she improves daily, and her life has never been the same. In recent years, Riley has been successfully teaching classes and conducting workshops to help others utilize special healing techniques revealed to her by her angel. Not only was she blessed with her own healing, her prayers to be an instrument of healing have also been granted, as she receives many confirmations that her healing methods are working for others. She has now become an instrument of angelic intelligence, blessed with the ability to teach others how to use their minds to heal their bodies.

*W*hen Marissa went to bed that September night in 1999, she wondered how much more she could possibly endure, and why so many burdens had been placed upon her. In addition, she wondered, as perhaps so many do, why God was picking on her.

Since childhood, Marissa had been taught by those in charge of her religious training that God was a distant, imposing male figure who was filled with vengeance and wrath.

"God seemed to me to be an ancient tribal god, fierce and demanding. I knew that God must have judged me guilty of something, but I couldn't figure out just what it was that I had done to so arouse his wrath against me."

Then, in the early predawn hours, Marissa was awakened by a bright light shining in her eyes. When she opened them, she saw a sphere of light about four feet in diameter, floating in her room.

"It was about six to eight feet from my bed," she said. "It looked like a luminous, wispy fog, and it was swirling within itself, very gently rotating from my right to left. I was immediately filled with a sense of great peace and tranquility. All of my troubled feelings immediately vanished. And then this sphere of light spoke to me."

A clear, soft male voice asked Marissa if she were afraid. After taking some moments to collect her mental equilibrium, she told the light being that she felt no fear.

"I was nearly overcome because he was radiating something of unspeakable beauty," she said. "I felt his light envelope me and flow through me. It was a light which was not limited by boundaries of physical matter. It was a light of great gentleness and compassion beyond words."

The light within, around, or generated by the benevolent being became even brighter as he spoke. "You are loved unconditionally," he said. "The Creator Spirit is not filled with wrath and vengeance as so many Earth religions have taught, but that which you call 'God' is pure love beyond comprehension. What you humans have mistaken as punishment from your fierce concept of God is nothing more than the effects of your own actions."

Marissa said that the light being placed great importance on the need for humans to begin to understand the relationship between cause and effect, because it was through this understanding that human spiritual evolution will occur.

"At this point," Marissa said, "the light coming from the celestial being went through me, and I experienced unconditional love for the first time in my life. It was searing—and exquisite. It was as though I was being bathed in a light that entered every cell in my body and filled everything it passed through with love.

"As the light washed through me, it removed all traces of fear, anxiety, guilt, and loneliness, and I felt clean and profoundly at peace. I began vibrating, as though to the sound of light, and I suddenly became aware of each cell in my body and I felt love and compassion for them."

The light being told her to open herself and fill herself with the energy that was emanating from him.

Marissa did as the being instructed her.

"Incredibly, as I allowed more of his light energy to flow through me, I felt filled, but knew that I could never truly be filled," she said. "And although he was filling my being with this incredible love, his own brilliant light was not diminishing. When I saw this, I knew the light was coming from a source that was endless and was equally available for all people. I knew that I was not being singled out; this same love was available for all of creation. And this realization only added to my elation, because there was great comfort in discovering that I was not a single entity, that I was a part of all creation. I was feeling joy, relief, peace, love beyond any level I ever thought the human body was capable of achieving."

The light being startled Marissa when he suddenly asked her to think of her worst enemy. She thought such a request to be an odd one in the midst of such illumination, but she did as she was asked, thinking of a male coworker who, for some unknown reason, had taken an instant dislike to her when she had started her new job. In addition, the man had spread the most horrible gossip and ugly rumors about her. Marissa had tried to speak to him and ask him what he could possibly have against her, but her attempt at some kind of reasonable resolution had been met with contempt and vicious words.

The light being then stated that humans were neither judged nor punished by the Creator Spirit; hatred, anger, prejudice, and ill will were creations of humankind and directed by those of low awareness toward their fellow men and women.

"Recognize the animosity that you feel toward this person, the anger with which you are filled toward your enemy," the light being commanded.

"I did this," Marissa said, "and saw a projection of my dislike of this person manifest in the form of a dark cloud. But as I was projecting this darkness, the illumination within me did not flicker or grow dim; I was still shining."

And then, she declared, something beautiful happened.

"Now surround this person with the golden light of love and forgiveness," the being told her. "Send the powerful light of forgiveness toward this person. Let him know that he, as are you, is a child of God, and that the great Power that spans the universe loves both of you."

"As the energy that I was projecting engulfed my image of the man and flowed through me, there was an explosion of light like the reflection of the sun in a mirror, and all that I had sent out to him suddenly returned to me.

"I was already filled and glowing, but now what I had sent out had also come back and filled me even further. Again, there was no way for me to express this sensation of wild joy. I wanted to sing with the light, although I had no breath."

Marissa was aware that she was sitting on the edge of her bed, tears running down her face, a smile on her lips. Slowly, her breath returned.

The light being waited in silence as Marissa recovered from an experience that she will remember and follow forever. Then, very quietly, he said, "You have just prayed for the first time in your life. You have forgiven another for ill will directed against you. You have replaced anger and hate with love and light. Teach others how to forgive those who trespass against them."

At that very moment, Marissa knew that somehow the animosity felt toward her by her coworker had been dissolved. She also knew that it had not been God that had been punishing her and filling her with feelings of guilt, but her own lack of awareness that had betrayed her into projecting hatred toward her coworker. She had been taught one of the most basic of spiritual lessons: Hatred destroys most the one who practices it and keeps it.

The next day at work, Marissa and the man who had been the object of her projected love and light of forgiveness nearly collided at the water cooler. Now, she thought to herself, she would soon see if her spiritual vision truly had a counterpart in the real world.

"Sorry," he said, stepping aside and allowing her to fill her cup first.

As Marissa was running the water, she heard him mumble something behind her back. Fearing the worst, she turned and asked him what he had said.

"I said I was sorry about not giving you a chance," he said. "I've been watching you; you're really a hard worker. I think someday you might make a contribution to the office."

Marissa thanked him, walked back to her desk, then thanked her angel for helping her learn to forgive and to turn her life around. True, her former nemesis hadn't embraced her and begged forgiveness, but it was a start. A good start.

*L*illian was going through a lot of emotional trauma, raising four sons alone, becoming financially desperate, beginning a new relationship that seemed uncertain. She was at the point where she was beginning to think that if there really was a God, He or She sure had a grudge against her for some reason. Maybe she had been an awful tyrant in some former life.

"I truly felt as though my kids hated me," Lillian said. "I know that their father had poisoned their minds against me. It had not been an amicable divorce, and lots of horrible words and awful accusations had been overheard by the children. My ex-husband, Hank, and I did not stay friends and wish each other well when the divorce was final. I didn't start seeing Max until five months later, but Hank told the kids that he was the reason that I broke up our marriage. And then Hank had been killed in an accident at the construction site where he worked."

Lillian kept hearing accusations of failure screaming through her brain whenever it was time for her to try to get some sleep: If she had been a better wife . . . If she had been a better mother . . . If she had been a better housekeeper . . . If she had been a better person . . . .

Even worse were the overwhelming feelings of guilt that she had somehow been responsible for Hank's death. Lillian kept hearing the anger in her oldest daughter's voice when she had shouted, "It's your fault Daddy died. He was so depressed over the divorce that he wasn't thinking right or concentrating on his work. That's why he had the accident!"

Lillian found no way to explain to her children, her parents, Hank's parents, or any other friends or family members that he had begun drinking heavily on weekends when he didn't work. He had been getting together with his buddies and binge drinking while they watched football games on Saturday and Sunday afternoons. When he finally got home, long after the children were sleeping, he had become increasingly abusive to Lillian. Lillian had kept Hank's alcohol abuse a secret from everyone in order to preserve his reputation, but now she felt like the guilty one for not insisting that Hank get help. Instead, she had filed for divorce.

Night after night, as she tossed and turned, unable to sleep, she had decided that she was doomed to be guilt-ridden forever.

Then one spring night in 2001, just as she was finally drifting off to sleep, something made Lillian open her eyes.

"I can still see the figure standing there in a robe, the hood closely draped around a darkly shadowed face, a rope loosely knotted around the waist," Lillian said. "The figure was about five-feet-eight, of slim to average build; and in the moonlight coming through my window and the illumination from the nightlight beside my dresser, its hands seemed olive complexioned."

At first, Lillian thought that she was being visited by the Angel of Death. After an initial feeling of fear, she became calmer and resigned to her fate.

"Part of me thought that it was some kind of messenger of God that had been sent to punish me for my sins," Lillian said. "If that was what it was, I decided, why fight it? It has me cornered; I can't escape. Let it do to me what it has been sent to do."

Lillian has no idea how much time passed, but it seemed as though the hooded being had been standing in her bedroom for at least five or ten minutes before it began to move toward her.

Again, Lillian admitted, she was frightened, but resolved to accept whatever actions the being had come to administer.

Then the mysterious visitor was standing next to her bed. Lillian tried to see its face, but she could perceive only a soft blue light emanating from beneath the dark cowl. The entity said nothing, but merely brought its hand very slowly close to hers so that the backs of their hands nearly touched.

"I think that our spirits, our auras, some indefinable level of consciousness must have mingled somehow, and that was the means of communication," Lillian said. "I have a hard time finding words to describe all of this, but at that moment, I was filled with a feeling of total and complete unconditional love. If there had been a gauge to have measured my heart and spirit, I would have been at maximum capacity. The forgiveness and the absolute divine lovingness that the figure was conveying brought tears to my eyes, and I had the feeling that this was but one molecule of one grain of sand in an entire universe of love. I felt that if the being were to turn up its love energy to full power, there could be no way in which my mind would ever be able to handle it. Then I fell asleep."

Lillian said that the visitation of the hooded entity brought her back to her senses spiritually, and the experience seemed to have been a turning point in her life.

"My spiritual balance was restored when that loving visitor filled my entire being with unconditional love," Lillian said. "Those terrible feelings of failure and the psychically crippling sense of guilt began to subside. In essence, I think that I had been told to 'let go, and let God.' I wish I could have seen the angel's face!"

With her spiritual equilibrium fully charged with love, Lillian was able to offer herself as a true partner to Max—a woman with self-esteem and strength. At the same time, she found the confidence to reveal the truth about their father to her children and, at the same time, the wisdom to allow them to love him for the good times and the good memories that he gave them. With a heart filled with the divine forgiveness bestowed upon her by the hooded figure, Lillian, too, would allow the physical and mental scars of abuse to fade into forgetfulness.

In September 1968, Charlie was blown out of a helicopter while attempting to land and pick up wounded soldiers at a remote base under attack in Vietnam. A rocket fired from the ground struck and severely damaged the helicopter and threw Charlie clear.

Charlie felt an arm around his shoulder, and in his head he heard a voice saying, "Charlie, trust me and lean on me, and I will be there with you always."

He watched the ground rushing toward him 100 feet below. Just before impact, he felt something squeeze him, then everything went black. Charlie was in and out of consciousness for several days. When he returned to full wakefulness, he found that, miraculously, he had somehow lived through the fall and had suffered no permanent injury.

In 1972, while employed by an Arkansas police department, Charlie was riding his motorcycle to work. He had just passed a semi truck when he got a flat tire. Charlie felt the bike shake and turn suddenly sideways. To his horror, he saw that he was sliding across the interstate toward the semi.

Once again, he heard the voice asking him to trust it. At the last second, Charlie's bike moved behind the rear dual on the trailer of the semi, slid onto a curb on the inside lane, sat upright, and rolled to a stop. An unseen "someone" beside him had steered the bike out of danger.

In 1984, Charlie responded to a burglar alarm at a business that had frequently sounded false alarms. It was almost 11:00 P.M., time for a shift change, and Charlie called off the backup unit, assuming that the signal would turn out to be another false alarm. He didn't even unholster his revolver when he arrived to check out the building.

When Charlie rounded the back corner of the building, he saw a hole knocked in the wall and a perpetrator standing there with merchandise from the business. At the same time, he saw the subject was reaching for a gun in his waistband.

Again, the voice: "Trust me, Charlie. I am here for you always."

Charlie will never forget how "something" behind him pushed him down on the ground while he was drawing his weapon. He heard two shots fired by the suspect just before he made his getaway. Later, Charlie found that the burglar's bullets had hit the wall just a foot to his right.

Charlie concluded his account by stating that the angel's promise to be with him always has come true many times. Anytime he ever felt alone or afraid, he has always felt the angel of the Lord beside him—never ahead or behind, but always beside him. Charlie knows without a doubt that his guardian angel will always be there for him.

*I*n the mid-1990s, Michelle, a licensed clinical social worker, was struggling to complete the requirements for state licensure for her clinical social work certification. Part of this training involved traveling to Seattle for consultation with a qualified clinical social worker who had a private psychotherapy practice.

"This happened once a week," she explained, "and involved getting up at about 4:30 A.M. to get ready to catch a ride with a friend who was in training/consultation with me. Then we'd drive the fifty-six miles to the ferry, leave the car, and walk aboard as foot passengers. Once in Seattle, we would walk the many blocks to our supervisor's office. When the meeting was over, we'd rush back to the ferry, cross Puget Sound, drive back to the Peninsula, and usually immediately go back to work. It was exhausting but necessary, and we were usually fairly tired most of the time."

The day she had her angelic encounter was warm and sunny, almost hot. She and her friend had left their consultation session, run to the ferry, and barely made it on board before the ferry pulled away from the dock.

"I got a cup of coffee," she recalled, "took a few unhurried breaths, and tried to relax. I was tired, slightly sweaty, and frazzled, weary from having to rush around all the time and work so hard. Everything seemed hard right then.

"I decided to use the bathroom before the ferry docked and we had to begin our ninety-minute drive home. While I was washing up in the bathroom, there was a minor commotion behind me. A young girl, about eight or nine years old, was trying to help her younger sister wash up. In the process, she had gotten water on the younger girl's dress.

"The little one screeched, and the mother began scolding the older girl loudly and severely for getting the little one damp. My heart went out to the older girl. She'd been doing her best to help a fairly unruly little sister and was being publicly humiliated for her efforts.

"When I dried my hands and turned around, I made a point of catching her eye and I gave her a big 'I think you are a cool kid' smile.

"Suddenly," Michelle recalled, "her face was transformed. Her eyes suddenly blazed with the truest sky blue, her face began to glow, and she gave me a smile that almost knocked me over! It literally took my breath away.

"As I turned around and walked away, I felt fifteen years younger and twenty pounds lighter. I walked back to the rear of the ferry in a sort of daze and told my friend, 'I think I just saw an angel.'

"She, of course, wanted to go find the little girl and see her. Somehow, I knew that wouldn't be the right thing to do, and I refused. I wasn't even positive that family was still on the ferry!"

Michelle admitted that she really didn't know what actually happened. "An angel suddenly peered out at me from behind that sweet and pretty little girl's face," she said. "It was a smile full of fierce love. It was *fierce*. That was the thing that stunned me. It wasn't a sweet smile; it was dazzling, brilliant, literally breathtaking, and it pierced me to the heart.

"The rest of my day, and indeed many days after that, were considerably lightened by that unexpected encounter," she said. "Since that day, I have wondered what she saw when she looked at me. I hope that my angel was smiling fiercely back at her!"

One night in 1995, Darlene, a single mother living alone with two small children, was gripped by fear when she heard strange noises outside her bedroom window.

Darlene walked cautiously toward the window, listening for movement outside, and peeked through the blinds.

Instead of an intruder attempting to break a window and invade her home, Darlene saw two remarkable beings illuminated in bright white light standing in her front yard.

Darlene said that although the two beings looked almost identical, each had his own distinct characteristics. "One was slightly taller than the other, and the shorter one had a softer appearance," she said, "while the taller one had a stern, almost intimidating, composure. They looked like two guards, watching, looking around, pacing back and forth.

Neither one of them looked at me, but I knew they could sense my presence. They knew I was looking through the blinds at them."

Darlene told us that she immediately felt an overwhelming peace that she had never before experienced. "Seeing these two beings standing in my front yard made me more comfortable than I'd ever felt," she said. "I didn't stop staring out the window for a very long time. I could not take my eyes off of them. I let every detail soak into my mind until I had a perfect mental picture of them. It was the most awesome experience of my entire life."

Darlene crawled back in bed with a big smile on her face. "I knew at that moment my prayers had been answered," she said. "I knew I was being protected by these heavenly beings sent from up above. After receiving this angelic assurance, I was able to sleep better at night, and I no longer walked around in constant fear."

Darlene admitted that she had not believed in angelic intervention until she actually saw proof that her guardian angels are always close, "barely a whisper away."

*H*ayden is convinced that he has traveled to another plane of existence in the company of his angelic guide and met with the spirits of his departed loved ones. Although he considers himself an active member of a large Protestant congregation in the Midwest, he has come to believe that the deceased continue to exist in Heaven in much the same manner as they did in life.

"I know that my belief may not harmonize exactly with church doctrine," Hayden admitted, "but I really believe that deep down inside we all cherish the belief that our departed loved ones are with the angels in Heaven. And I know in my spirit that I have been there and spoken with my departed loved ones."

In his report to us, Hayden said that he first had the experience of visiting the heavenly realms when his dear sister passed away. He had been practicing meditation for years, and on occasion was convinced that he had the ability to project his soul essence in what is commonly called an out-of-body experience. Because he missed his sister so much, it seemed logical to Hayden that he might travel in his soul body to visit her in Heaven.

Hayden surrounded himself with light and asked for angelic guidance. Within a short time, he said, his angel guide appeared.

"It was as if I had always been aware of his existence on one level of my consciousness," Hayden said. "He appeared to me in the robes of a priest, which would be consistent with my religious orientation. His countenance was magnificent. When he reached out and took my hand, I felt as though electricity was flowing through my spirit body."

It seemed to Hayden that the next moment he and his angel guide were standing within a lovely courtyard. Hayden looked around and saw what appeared to be grape arbors, olive trees, and a host of other splendid trees, vines, and flowers. He knew this had to be his sister Victoria's idea of Heaven.

Hayden's guide nodded approval at his deduction, and within a few moments, his sister Victoria joined them in the courtyard. She seemed surprised to see Hayden, but she came immediately to embrace her brother. Hayden was elated to see that her arrival in

Paradise had eliminated all traces of the ravages of her cancer.

Hayden said that tears came to his eyes when he told her that they had not had the time to say a proper farewell to one another. She agreed that this was so.

"In the summer of 1999, Victoria's chemotherapy seemed to be making progress in defeating the cancer," Hayden said. "It was my turn at the clinic to take a holiday, and my fiancée and I were interested in joining a tour group that would visit Peru. Both Victoria and her husband Lonny encouraged us to go, saying that things were taking a turn for the better. As the good Lord would have it, things took a terrible turn for the worst."

Lonny's desperate telephone messages didn't catch up with Hayden until they had returned from a visit to Machu Picchu and were staying in a hotel in Cusco. It was difficult obtaining a flight back to the States on short notice, and Hayden said that he would always recall the anguish and helplessness that he suffered during those three days that it took to book a flight back to Tampa.

Hayden said that he arrived shortly after Victoria had lapsed into the coma from which she never awoke. Family members promised him that she was aware that he was doing his best to be there at her bedside, but such assurances never comforted him.

"In that time with Victoria in that heavenly garden, we were able to say the words to each other that we had not been able to say back on Earth," Hayden said. "I cannot gauge how long I was actually in that celestial place; it seemed a few hours or more, but I know that I was blessed to be in a place where time as we measure it does not exist."

Although the time that he was able to spend with Victoria was deeply meaningful to him, Hayden was saddened when his angel guide indicated that it was time to return to his physical body on Earth. His sorrow proved fleeting, however, when his guide assured Hayden that he had the ability to return in his soul body to communicate with Victoria. Hayden truly felt transformed, and greatly elevated in body, mind, and spirit.

Since that time, Hayden said, he has traveled time and again to Heaven and talked with departed loved ones. "I have also met the spirits of many individuals whom I did not know in life," he added. "In many instances, I have recorded their names and former addresses immediately upon returning to my body. In each case, my subsequent investigations have determined the reality of their lives on Earth, and whenever possible, I have contacted their living loved ones with their messages from Heaven."

*J*ames went for a long walk—a kind of meditation in motion, he called it—when he learned that his mother might not recover from her most recent heart attack. As it was growing dark, he approached the small creek in the forest where he had spent so much time as a boy and was amazed to see two glowing figures sitting on the bank.

As his eyes adapted to the darker hues of nightfall, he could clearly distinguish two angels.

"They didn't have wings," he said, "but they definitely fit the classic descriptions of angels that I had heard or read about since I was a child. The most peculiar aspect of my experience is thinking that those angels were just kind of hanging out, like they were taking a break from the serious business of watching over the world by relaxing on the bank of the creek."

After the surprise of seeing angels wore off, James said that his next thought was that they had come to tell him that his mother had died. As he began to walk toward the angels, they seemed to become much brighter in appearance, and the entire landscape around them seemed to become one with their light.

James suddenly saw the image of his mother standing next to the two angels. He shouted and began to run toward them.

One of the angels stood up and extended an outstretched palm toward James, signaling him to stop. His mother turned to smile at him, and he was startled to see how young and beautiful she looked; she looked just like she did when he was a little boy.

"I felt then as though I were being held in suspended animation," James said. "A voice spoke to me as if coming from an echo chamber and told me to be still and watch. Somehow, I was led to understand that what I was about to see was for my benefit."

As James watched, silent and immobile, he observed a kind of projection of what he knew was to be a future reality.

His mother took the hand of one of the angels and began to walk toward a bright light. The other angel joined them, and the three of them went into the light. James felt a wave of euphoric, unconditional love and a sense of completeness wash over him.

Next, James sensed, more than saw, his mother and the angels in a heavenly realm. Men and women crowded around his mother, and James recognized some of them as family members that had already passed away. He was certain that he saw the spirit of his father move forward and embrace his mother.

And then the brightly lit scene was gone, and James stood alone in the darkness.

James ran back to the gravel road where he had parked his car and drove immediately to the hospital where his mother lay dying. He knew that the vision presaged his mother's final moments.

When he entered the room, his two sisters embraced him tearfully. "Thank God, you're here," his older sister Camryn said. "Mother lapsed into unconsciousness, and the doctors are saying that she's just shutting down. It's best if we let her go; she's been through enough suffering."

"We know how hard you've taken Mom's illness," Caroline said. "We know how much you've dreaded this moment; but it has come. We have to face it."

James told them that he was at peace with their mother's passing because he had been shown that she would soon be in a beautiful place with loved ones and benevolent beings.

As they held hands, bowed their heads, and prayed beside their mother's bedside, James became convinced that he had been granted a vision of a kind of celestial dress rehearsal to comfort him and assure him that his mother would find peace on the other side.

"Mom passed that night shortly after midnight," James said, "and later that night, as I slept, I had a very interesting dream."

Once again, in his dream, James was standing in a cloudlike fog beside the creek in the forest. He was met by an elder being with a white beard, who was dressed in a white, flowing robe. The being took James's hand and they floated to the top of a high hill.

"We looked down upon a very beautiful city of light that had a temple with a golden dome in its center," James said. "The temple was shining very brightly, and surrounding the entire city was a beautiful, soft, peaceful, loving, yellowish-white, gold light that I knew emanated from God."

The elder being looked into James' eyes and said, "It is as your mother wished. She is in a Heaven that has a city made of gold. Even the streets are made of gold."

James said that he would always remember the being's final words to him in the dream: "As you live your life on Earth, keep always in mind that the Light of God is brighter and more precious than all the gold in Heaven or Earth. The Love of God can outshine all illumination in the universe."

$\mathcal{G}$ race told us that she first met her guardian angel when she nearly died of pneumonia at the age of three.

"I remember so clearly the image of a beautiful blue-white angel lady who stayed with me throughout the entire period of the illness," Grace said. "Whenever I opened my eyes, she would be there at the side of my bed, smiling at me. Sometimes I heard her humming this lovely melody, the beauty of which I have never heard reproduced by anyone on this level of consciousness."

As a child, Grace became aware of other angel guides, and her ability to leave the physical body and travel to Heaven.

"By the time I was a teenager," she said, "I regularly traveled to the higher planes to meet with the spirits of family and others who had passed on."

Such cosmic travel had become so natural for Grace that she knew when the time came for her to make the final, ultimate trip to Heaven, she would already know her way around. She wouldn't have to go through the period of adjustment that so many individuals have to go through when they leave their physical bodies behind in death.

In 2000, Grace was involved in a two-way traffic collision that proved fatal for her mother, who was sitting in the passenger side of the front seat.

Although she was badly injured, she said that she was conscious when she saw the beautiful blue-white angel lady who had visited her when she was ill as a child come to take her mother's spirit by the hand.

"I was able to say goodbye to Mother and watch her ascend with my guardian angel into the heavenly light," Grace said. "Although some may scoff at me, I believe that my soul essence has since visited my mother and the blue-white angel lady many times since Mother's translation to Heaven."

*I*n 2001, at the beginning of his junior year in college, a disillusioned Dylan was seriously contemplating dropping out and getting a job with his uncle's trucking firm.

"I had just about decided that I was not cut out to be a scholar," Dylan said. "I had enrolled in college after I had graduated from high school, became discouraged, and dropped out after my sophomore year. I worked for my father in his warehouse business for two years, met Maggie, and got married. She and Dad encouraged me to go back to college and complete my degree, but I resisted, until they finally talked me into enrolling and trying it again at the local college."

It was only the second week of classes when Dylan's father suffered a massive heart attack and died while checking on a load of merchandise at the warehouse. Dylan admitted that his father's death was a "real downer," and that he had never realized just how much his father's guidance and advice had meant to him. The grim fact of his father's death had also driven home the reality that life is short and that you must be thoughtful and cautious when making decisions that may be life altering.

Dylan said that taking a nice long hike around the lake had always helped him clear his mind.

"I was walking across campus when I noticed this guy watching me from the shadow of a large oak tree next to the gym," Dylan said. "He was a tall, fairly well-built man with long blond hair. Later, as I cut through the city park, I saw him again, like he was following me. That evening, when I was checking out some supplementary reading in the campus library, I saw him again. I was about to approach him and ask him what was the deal. Was he following me?"

That night, Dylan was awakened by a bright light shining at the foot of his bed. Maggie was sound asleep, and somehow he knew that he would not be able to awaken her.

"I had to squint into the light it was so bright," Dylan said. "Then I saw that a human shape was beginning to form within the light. I assumed that it had to be an angel to be surrounded by such brilliant illumination. After a few more moments, another form became visible, and I was astonished to see my father standing side by side with an angelic being. I was equally astonished to see that the angel was the same guy with the long blond hair that had been following me around that day."

Dylan's father told him not to be frightened, and that he had asked permission of the angels to visit him to encourage him to return to college and complete the degree that he had abandoned five years before. He also asked Dylan to be more attentive toward his stepmother and to help her make the adjustment over his sudden passing.

"When I asked Dad about the angel escort," Dylan said, "his answer was simple: 'I was afraid I couldn't get down to Earth and back to Heaven by myself.'"

Dylan burst out laughing. That was just like his father's wry sense of humor.

At the sound of his laughter, Dylan's father and the angel escort vanished, and Maggie awakened.

"What's the matter, Hon?" she asked, yawning and glancing at the time on the alarm clock. "Is it time to wake up?"

Dylan told her that it most certainly was time for him to wake up to a new frame of consciousness: He would stay in college and complete the degree that his father had always wanted him to attain. He also told her that he felt that they had been neglecting his stepmother lately, and that they should take her out for dinner that Sunday.

Maggie threw her arms around Dylan, and wondered aloud what had brought about this sudden marvelous change in attitude. Respectfully, she listened to Dylan tell about how his guardian angel had brought his father back down to Earth for a life-altering conversation.

_G_loria, a respondent to our Steiger Question-naire of Mystical and Paranormal Experi-ences from San Antonio, reported her near-death experience while under the surgeon's scalpel.

Gloria stated that she could clearly see her body below her, but she didn't really want to watch the surgeons working on her, so she did not resist when she felt a force pulling her higher, farther away from the operating room where skilled physicians were dealing with complications of her intestinal-cancer surgery.

She thought of her husband and her three-year-old daughter in the waiting room, and she felt sad that she was leaving them, for she was convinced that she was dying. But she also knew that she would no longer have to feel any more sickness or pain.

She heard bells tolling, like they do after funerals; and then Gloria saw her guardian angel coming

down through the ceiling to take her hand.

The angelic being accompanied Gloria toward a bright light that appeared to be shining in the center of a great expanse of darkness.

Gloria felt herself blending with the powerful energy of the light, and it seemed as if her very essence was being separated, layer by layer. "It was wonderful!" she recalled. "Like each layer of my essence was being bathed in soft, warm soapy love."

The next thing Gloria knew, she had on a lovely white robe, and all around her were beautiful angels in bright, shining gowns. The angelic beings seemed to be glowing with an inner radiance.

And then, Gloria believed that she had been blessed beyond comprehension when a magnificent angel, very feminine in appearance, manifested before her. "Because I was a devout Roman Catholic, I thought that I was beholding Mother Mary," Gloria told us. "This beautiful feminine figure was standing in the midst of a group of angels, and I fell to my knees and began to weep."

The glorious angel spoke to Gloria in a soft, gentle voice and informed her that although she was not the being that Gloria had at first supposed, she was her guardian angel, who had been near Gloria since her birth. The angel went on to tell Gloria that her stay would be brief, then she must return to Earth.

Gloria remembers asking the angel her name.

The heavenly being smiled. "What you mean by someone's name has no meaning to us. Angels seldom give humans their names. There is much power in an angel's name; know this and understand this, for great disasters may ensue from misusing holy names."

Another angel added, "Another reason that we rarely provide our names is due to the human failing of attempting to worship us or to call us to do their bidding. We are never to be worshipped, for to God alone is the glory. And we are not to be summoned for such low-level activities as magic or sorcery."

Gloria was confused: Was she never to be able to call upon her angels for strength or guidance?

"You must never make unwise demands of us," she was told. "The lessons of life are best learned if you learn to make use of your own resources, thus rising to greater strength by so doing. We are always with you, providing you with inspiration and guidance from the unseen dimensions. But we are not to accomplish your lessons for you."

Gloria's guardian told her that since the name seemed to mean so much to her, Gloria might call her "Mary."

Her guardian, "Mary," motioned to Gloria to follow her, and she and the group of angelic beings walked to a beautiful area of flowers, green grass, and a small stream. When the angels rested near a large tree, they formed a small circle around Gloria.

"Although you have become one with the light here on one of the heavenly spheres," Mary said to Gloria, "you have always walked in the spiritual light, even while you were on Earth. When we angels come down to your material sphere, we can easily see which of you humans have the spiritual light within you."

Another angel spoke up and told her that it was such beacons of light that aided them in finding their way while on Earth. "And such lights certainly help us to find those to whom we are assigned to minister."

Gloria acknowledged that she had always tried to be a good Catholic.

Mary smiled. "Yes, my child, that is fine. But the spiritual light does not belong exclusively to any single religious expression."

Gloria was told what a privilege it was that she had been permitted to advance to the Greater Light and to become one with its beauty.

"The beauty of this Light is the beauty of Holiness," one of the benevolent beings said. "It is past the imagining of mortals, but it can also be attained by a regular practice of meditation and prayer. And be certain to keep a memory of the Light in your mind when things become difficult on Earth."

Speaking of things being difficult on Earth, Gloria asked the angels why, since Earth was going through such terrible times, the angels didn't appear as often to humans as they did in Biblical times.

One of the heavenly beings was quick to answer. "Angels rarely come to the earth plane with the intention of 'appearing' to humans. We work always for humans and are present always in some dimension of being, but we seldom visibly appear in our actual forms. We may assume other physical identities—we may even temporarily occupy the physical being of another human—but we may not appear as angelic beings unless it be for some very rare and special assignment."

Gloria said that she understood, then commented on the beauty of Heaven and how wonderful it was to be able to receive such a blessing.

"This is not the true Heaven," one of the angels cautioned her. "This is a construct that we have created for your learning. It is our intention that this experience will contribute greatly to the positive growth of your soul."

"But enough of our instructions," Mary smiled. "We know that while you are here on the outer edge of Heaven, you would like to see someone."

"My parents!" Gloria exclaimed.

Gloria said that in another "twinkling of an eye," her parents, Manuel and Felicia, manifested before her.

They all wept tears of joy at their heavenly reunion. Gloria took note of the fact that neither of her parents looked as old as they had at their time of physical death. Both of them appeared as she remembered them from her childhood.

In the account of her visit to Heaven that Gloria wrote later, she observed that it seemed as though she spent two or three days visiting with her parents in the angelic realm.

Then Mary, her angelic guardian, knocked at the door of the lovely little house where Gloria and her parents had been staying and told her that it was time to return. At Mary's side was the same angel who had ascended with Gloria into the Light.

"No sooner had my guardian angel spoken these words than I was bobbing near the ceiling of a hospital room," Gloria said. "I was shocked to hear Father Sanchez below me, giving my body the last rites. My husband lay across my feet crying, and I somehow knew that my sister was outside in the hall with my daughter. A nurse stood at the left side of the bed, her fingers on my pulse."

At this point, Gloria said that she received another image of Mary, her guardian angel. "You could only stay with us for a little while," Mary said. "It was not yet your time to remain, but remember well all the lessons that you have received in the heavenly realm."

There was a strange, crackling noise, and Gloria realized after a few moments that she was back in her physical body.

"I moaned with the pain of my illness and the surgery," Gloria said. "When I opened my eyes, my husband and Father Sanchez were smiling, and the nurse had just reentered the room with our doctor."

Gloria weakly found her voice and told them that she had been to Heaven and had spoken with angels.

Father Sanchez said that he did not doubt that she had gone somewhere far away, for the doctors at the hospital had only given her a few minutes more to either pass the crisis point or to pass on to another world. He had been called upon to administer the last rites, because her chances to live had seemed very slim.

"Our doctor told us that the surgeon had been certain that she had been able to remove all the cancer and that it should be a good long time before I returned to Heaven," Gloria said, concluding her story. "Before my heavenly journey, I had been a very materialistic person. Now I realized that there was far more to life than shopping at the best stores, eating at the best restaurants, and looking great for the country club dances. I became a volunteer at the hospice and sought to assure those who suffered there that a greater world awaited them."

*L*awrence, an attorney, recalled the night in 1996 when he was working late doing research for a particularly difficult case. He at first heard a strange humming sound, and when he glanced up, he saw what appeared to be a shimmering light in the corner of his office. As he directed his attention to the light, he was astonished to see it take the form of Tyler, his deceased younger brother, who had died three months earlier in a hunting accident.

Lawrence insists that he was wide awake, but suddenly he felt as if he were being pulled out of his body, as if his very soul were somehow being drawn out through the top of his skull.

"The image of my brother reached out his hand to me, and suddenly I was at his side, clasping the hand that I had so often held in life," Lawrence said. "I looked back toward the desk and saw my physical body sitting slumped over, staring at some papers.

My eyes were open, but I seemed to be in some kind of trance."

Lawrence said that he became very frightened. He had no idea how such things could be. Had the ghost of his younger brother come to claim his soul and take him with him into the grave? But such an act would be a malignant one, an evil one; he and Tyler had always loved each other and there had never been any dissension between them.

And then, Lawrence became aware that a tall man dressed in a brilliant white suit was standing there with them.

"There is no question in my mind now, and there was no doubt then, that the being was an angel," Lawrence said. "His eyes seemed to penetrate my very soul. You know, this is strange, but I can't remember if his mouth opened and closed when he spoke, but I surely heard his words inside my very essence: 'You must come with us for a little while.'"

Lawrence felt as if he were spinning, and everything went black.

"But it was only dark for a second or two," he said, "then the three of us were standing on the side of a mountain. It seemed like we were somewhere in Colorado, but I'm sure we were someplace even higher than the Rockies."

Tyler was still holding on to Lawrence's hand, and he squeezed it hard when he spoke to him. Tyler beseeched Lawrence to promise that he would look after his five-year-old son, Evan. "You must promise me," Tyler demanded. "You must begin to spend a lot of time with him. He's only a little kid. He can't handle my dying and all."

Lawrence told his brother that he was surprised that he would have to ask such a thing. "You know I will take care of Evan as if he were my own."

Tyler told him that was why he had brought an angel with him to record his brother's vow. "You're so busy building your law career you don't spend enough time with your own wife and kids; you certainly wouldn't find time for little Evan. You know that your wife is thinking about leaving you. You didn't even take the afternoon off when your baby girl was born last month. You probably don't even know the birthdays of your two other kids, 'cause you weren't at the hospital when they were born, either."

Lawrence looked from the pleading eyes of his brother to the stern, unyielding eyes of the big angel. "Make your vow," the angelic being said in a voice that vibrated within Lawrence's soul. "Make your vow so your brother may enter the Light of Heaven in peace."

Lawrence felt tears come to his eyes. "I promise, Tyler. I swear to all that's holy that I'll be like a father to your son. And I promise I'll be a better father to my own kids and a better husband to my wife."

Tyler kissed him on the cheek and gave him a hug, and for the first time since he joined them, the big angel smiled.

"Thanks, brother," Tyler said, as his image began to fade into shimmering light.

Just before Tyler disappeared, Lawrence heard him whisper to tell Sandy, his wife, and Evan that he would always love them.

"There was a moment or two of that spinning sensation, and when I regained consciousness, I was resting my head on my arms folded across the top of the desk," Lawrence said. "The whole episode couldn't have taken more than a minute or so, but it felt as though I had been somewhere else for a long time."

Lawrence said that he was very troubled after the experience, and it didn't matter to him whether it was a vision or an actual visitation from his brother and his guardian angel. Years later, the attorney is not at all interested in convincing others of the reality of the experience.

"I know it happened, and that it was a life-altering event in my life," he said. "I am not certain in what dimension the experience occurred, but I am forever grateful that it did occur, and I know it was real."

Lawrence left his office to return to his wife and kids as soon as he had recovered his equilibrium from the remarkable visitation. On the drive home, he made another promise to Tyler and the angel that he would keep his vow.

Lawrence's mystical experience occurred nearly twelve years ago, and he made good on his promises. He said that he and his wife grew closer again, and that he made the time to spend with his kids, no matter what.

"We included Evan and his mother in every family outing that we did," Lawrence said. "I took all the kids fishing every chance I got, and my wife and I attended all the kids' school and other activities. My children are all grown now, and I am even twice a grandpa. Evan is a senior in high school. He wants to teach high school, just like his father did."

Lawrence said that the experience with Tyler and the guardian angel remains as vivid in his mind as if it happened yesterday. "The whole experience seems to be set forever in my soul," he said, "as if it were a moment sealed in eternity."

*F*lorence had suffered from bronchial asthma ever since she was very young. One night in December 2002, when she was twenty-eight, she was standing before a mirror in her bedroom, trying on the evening dress she had splurged on for her husband's office New Year's Eve party. Florence had a thing about trying on anything in stores. Her husband jokingly accused her of making a game out of buying apparel in a store, then trying it on at home and returning it if she didn't like the way it looked.

As she stood before the mirror, smoothing a wrinkle here and there, she suddenly became aware of another face in the looking glass.

"It was that of a beautiful woman," Florence said. "She was surrounded by a lovely bluish-white aura, and she smiled at me before she spoke. 'You will soon be well,' she said."

Suddenly, Florence felt very dizzy and faint, and she rushed to lie down across the bed. She was having a terrible asthma attack, and felt as if hot pokers were stabbing her lungs. Before she could call out to her husband, she felt herself slipping into unconsciousness.

"I remember clearly feeling that the real part of me, I guess you would say my soul, just seemed to float above that poor wheezing body on the bed," Florence said. "I was concerned that the physical me couldn't breathe, but on the other hand, I had never experienced such a wonderful sense of freedom."

Florence felt herself drifting, floating upward. She seemed to pass through the ceiling of her room, and she was soon looking down on their neighborhood.

Then everything became rather surreal, and she felt as though she were drifting into another dimension of time and space. Ahead, she could see what looked like a tunnel through which she knew she must pass. There seemed to be a force that began to tug and pull at her. She became concerned that it might not be a good thing to be pulled into the tunnel.

During those first moments of anxiety, Florence recalled that she was surrounded by a bright light that just seemed to appear, then wrap itself around her. In the distance, she could see a city that appeared to be made of crystal. The sunlight reflected off roofs and towers, and it seemed a magnificent place. Florence knew with all her heart that she wanted to enter the city. Even from a distance, she could feel love—perfect love—emanating from its walls.

When Florence began to take a few steps on a pathway that led to the crystal city, the beautiful light that had enveloped her suddenly swirled into the form of the lovely lady in the mirror.

The heavenly being was now attired in a brilliant white robe. She appeared somewhat stern in her facial expression, but Florence could feel her very presence projecting feelings of unconditional love. Although the beautiful lady did not have the familiar wings that angels bore in Christmas displays, she still looked exactly the way Florence somehow knew that angels should.

"Although the crystal city is lovely, and I know that you are admiring it, you're not ready to go there," the angel said in a voice that seemed to vibrate within Florence's soul essence.

"I feel I belong there," Florence said. "I feel as though it is my true home."

The angel only smiled, then indicated that she should look at a crystal that she held in an outstretched hand.

"She moved the crystal over my chest," Florence said. "Strangely, I seemed to feel a marvelous energy suffusing both my soul essence and my physical body. I don't know how else to explain it."

The angel held the crystal up, and when she brought it down once again to the level of Florence's chest, there seemed to be a ray of golden light that emanated from the crystal into the very cells of Florence's lungs.

"The next thing that I was aware of," Florence said, "was waking up on our bed. My husband was there, holding my hand. He insisted upon taking me to the emergency room to be checked."

Later, when they were consulting with a doctor at the ER, she asked Florence about the inhaler that she had brought with her.

Florence explained that she had suffered from asthma since she was a child.

The doctor frowned as if puzzled and listened again to Florence's lungs. "Your lungs do seem a bit congested," she said, "but I would never have diagnosed you as having asthma."

Florence said that in another year she ceased using her inhaler altogether.

"I don't know why I was blessed with such a healing from the angels," she said. "I had decided not to have children because of my severe asthma. I am now pregnant. Perhaps my child will be a special person who will do the work of the angels on Earth. Or perhaps I may discover that my true mission is to preach of the wonders of angelic blessings."

*I*n spite of her surgeon's dire pronouncement that the cysts and lumps detected in her body were very likely cancerous, Beverly Hale Watson was healed by an angel on the night she awaited surgery in the hospital.

As Beverly describes the miracle, "Instantly there appeared at the foot of my bed a light being, whose brilliance was like the sun. I felt tremendous love projecting toward me. At the same time, a surge of heat entered through the crown of my head, shot through my body, and exited my feet, leaving behind an inner peace that has never left me."

When the doctors operated on Beverly the next morning, they were mystified to find nothing. Of course, Beverly was ecstatic to hear the medical confirmation that a miracle had taken place the night before, but she decided against telling her doctors about her "visitor," for fear they may have her transferred to the psychiatric floor for evaluation.

About three weeks after she was sent home from the hospital, Beverly noticed that she was beginning to know things that were going to happen to people. She also appeared to know things about certain people's past, things they might not wish others to know. The more she responded to the information coming from her inner voice, the more messages she began to receive telepathically—until they seemed to come nonstop. At that point, Beverly conveyed to the invisible source that she needed a better and more complete understanding of the mental transformation that was taking place within her.

Many years would pass before Beverly had another visit from a light being that manifested in completely visible form, but over the years she counted herself privileged to behold so many aspects of the Kingdom of the Lord, including those who are of "His/Her flock which we know not." She acknowledges that she has also learned the truth of the ancient warning, "Be careful what you ask for, because you just may get it!"

Beverly said that over the years, she has had numerous contacts with angels. "They have appeared as men, women, and children. We've met in grocery stores, restaurants, on airplanes, at sacred sites, to name only a few places. Each of God's messengers just seemed to show up at the exact moment that

I needed information, protection, or help. At other times, they were invisible to my eye, but I could feel their presence—especially when I visited hospital patients, ministered to individuals in crisis situations, or felt the death of a loved one was imminent.

"Since I beheld the light being as I sat on my hospital bed, God has shown me that we never walk alone during our time on Earth. Heavenly representatives of the Light are always available to us, simply for the asking."

Beverly said that most of the spiritual information that she receives from her guides comes through thoughts, ideas, intuitions, dreams, and visions. While she may not actually see her source, Beverly states that her body is very sensitive to vibrations or energies that are around her.

"I can sense when my cosmic friends are nearby," she said. "Sometimes, these Messengers of Light dress in feathers or fur and manifest as birds—especially hawks and crows—and cats and dogs. Their messages are conveyed to me telepathically, and I am able to respond in like manner."

Beverly has worked at many different kinds of jobs, but it was during her tenure with the Salvation Army that she heard the quiet voice of the Holy Spirit whisper that it was time to move on to another assignment. Assuming her new adventure would be in the corporate world, Beverly gave her two weeks' notice and left her position with the Salvation Army.

On a Monday morning in 1987, as she started to get out of bed, she was quite astonished to hear Spirit's new plans for her: "From this day forward, my child, you shall work for Me full time, writing My words."

Later that day, when she was working at her computer, a message came through to clear the screen. "Beautiful thoughts permeated my consciousness," she recalled. "Words began to flow through me that I knew were not of my mind. I couldn't believe the speed at which my fingers could type without errors. I had started my new job for Spirit with an exhilarating experience!"

Beverly was told that her first book would be one of poetry. Each poem would deal with life situations, and the title would be *Reflections of the Heart*. The person who would be responsible for the graphics and book layout would be Cynthia Seymour Hyder, a friend of hers, who had also worked with gifts of the Holy Spirit.

Since 1987, Beverly Hale Watson has been the vessel through which ten other books have been written. In addition, her inspired stories and messages have appeared in seventeen books by other authors.

In 1988, the Voice told her to form a nonprofit foundation to be called The Sevenfold Peace Foundation, and that its bylaws and mission statement would be written by Spirit. The foundation's mission would be to publish and distribute books, provide a newsletter, and offer intuitive counseling, educational classes, and materials to individuals on their evolutionary path to spiritual awakening.

In 1999, one of the foundation's major outreach programs included establishing a prison library containing religious and spiritual books at a facility in Colorado.

Today, Beverly Hale Watson of Double Oak, Texas, is the highly respected author of eleven inspirational works, including such memorable titles as *Messages from the Dove, Keys to the Book of Revelation, Reflections of the Heart,* and *Death: Our Portal to Life.*

"The greatest book you'll ever read," Beverly advises, "is the 'Book of Silence.' It is available to everyone who can stop the constant chatter of the mind. Within its pages, one may discover the keys to universal truth, wisdom, knowledge, and understanding. It is in your meditative moments that the Voice within can be heard. People go to God with an assortment of prayers, requesting assistance, answers, guidance, miracles, and so forth. They do all the talking, failing to remember that they can't hear the answers to their problems if they don't take the time to listen.

"Ask your angel guide, your Messenger of Light, to provide you with information that will be for your highest good. A few minutes of your time spent in silence can make the greatest difference in your reality. Messages will come to you in thoughts, ideas, intuitions, dreams, or visions."

Offering a last bit of advice to those still pondering their true mission on Earth, Beverly said, "Your soul knows why you are on Earth at this point in time. The answers to all your questions can be found simply by turning within. Follow your heartfelt feelings, act upon your thoughts and ideas, take notice when the subtle chills run down your spine or the hair on your arms stand on end. It is Spirit speaking to you. By following this Divine guidance, you will discover your mission."

*L*inda will never forget the day when her sixty-eight-year-old grandfather had a heart attack while driving in heavy traffic. She was ten, and the only passenger in his car. The only visible one, that is, as Linda watched luminous hands take control of the steering wheel and drive the car to safety.

"Everyone gave me the credit, of course," Linda, now in her mid-thirties, said. "No one really believed me when I said that an angel grabbed the wheel and got us to safety. The official explanation that satisfied everyone was that I had ridden in a car often enough to know how to get us out of traffic. No one considered that I was on the passenger side and that Grandpa, a pretty good-sized man, had fallen against me, thereby making it impossible for me to reach the steering wheel, the brake, or the accelerator. The theory with which everyone felt most comfortable was

Angel *Miracles*   119

that I managed to push Grandpa aside, grab the wheel, and weave in and out of rush hour traffic in Phoenix, Arizona. Emergency vehicles arrived and got Grandpa to the hospital in time to save his life, so I became a local hero for a couple of weeks. For months afterward, my friends called me Maria Andretti, in honor of the famous race car driver, Mario, and all through high school some kids wondered why my nickname was Andy, in homage to Andretti."

For those willing to hear what really happened that day, Linda describes the fear and helplessness that she felt when her grandfather clutched his chest, made an awful cry of pain, and fell against her. She had never driven a car. Her parents never indulged the ten year old and allowed her to sit behind the wheel when they were driving. Her father had always grumped that she would get her license and be driving too soon to suit him.

Linda remembers screaming, "Oh, dear God and holy angels, help me!"

Although Linda's family were regular churchgoers, she said that her concept of angels at that time consisted mostly of images of those featured in displays at Christmastime, intermingled with elves and red-nosed reindeer.

"I did not really see too much of the angel who took over the steering wheel," she said. "Mostly I saw these two big, luminous hands. I knew that they belonged to someone very strong, for one of them cradled Grandpa while the other muscled our car through traffic and pulled into the driveway of a gas station."

In 2003, Linda's angel with the powerful hands came into her life once again when her daughter Jenna was about fifteen months old.

"I was doing Yoga meditation in our recreation room," she said. "I had assumed a posture that bent my legs under me. Although I had retained a certain amount of muscular and joint flexibility, it still required a certain fair amount of time for me to unbend. I was certainly no gymnast who could unwind from the posture and leap to my feet."

She knew that she had left Jenna napping on a large pillow in the living room, but peculiar kitchen sounds were beginning to penetrate her meditative quiet.

Almost simultaneously with the intrusive sounds, Linda felt a powerful force suddenly lift her straight up and place her on her feet. Before she could absorb this incredible phenomenon of levitation, she felt a strong hand push against her back and propel her forward toward the kitchen. As if that weren't enough for her to deal with in this strangely altered reality, a powerful luminous hand clamped itself around her wrist and literally pulled her into the kitchen.

"Fortunately, I managed to retain my balance as the glowing hands pushed me into the kitchen," Linda said. "It was then that I saw little Jenna, who was supposed to be napping while I did my Yoga meditation, standing beside the kitchen sink. She had opened the cabinet doors, and was in the process of lifting a plastic container of Drano to her mouth. My entire essence was filled with horror as I recalled how I had left the difficult-to-unscrew cap merely sitting on top of the bottle to make it easier to use whenever it was time to unclog the drain. If it had not been for the angelic hands pulling and pushing me into the kitchen, Jenna would likely have swallowed the highly dangerous liquid in another few seconds."

Linda immediately implemented her too-long neglected resolution to childproof all cabinets, doors, and drawers that might contain harmful chemicals or sharp objects. Then, shuddering with the terrible thought of what might have happened had Jenna drunk from the bottle of poison, Linda gave thanks to her unseen angel guardian with the powerful hands.

When Ella was seven years old, she was surprised when her grandmother visited her on the playground at morning recess.

"Grandma Ava only lived a couple of blocks from the school, but she had never come by at recess time," Ella said. "She always came to us kids' school plays at Christmas with Mom and Dad, but it just wouldn't have been proper by our family rules to come around school when it was in session."

Ella remembers that she was playing jump rope with her friends when she saw Grandma Ava standing by the swings with a beautiful lady dressed in a gold gown. Grandma Ava was smiling, and she motioned for Ella to come to her.

Ella asked what Grandma Ava was doing there: Was something wrong with Mommy? Did something happen to Daddy at work? Was it Tommy or Karen? Or Uncle Melvin and Aunt Millie?

"No, no, no," Grandma Ava said. "They're all okay. I just wanted to stop by and see you."

Ella was puzzled; why hadn't she waited until after school?

Grandma Ava said that her friend had come for her and that she had to leave with her right away—she couldn't wait until school was over.

For the first time, Ella noticed her grandmother's friend—the tall, beautiful woman in the gold dress. If she was a friend of Grandma Ava's, she certainly had never seen her before. She had never seen her at Grandma's house when the ladies had their card parties.

"Hi," Ella said, minding her manners. "My name is Ella. What's yours?"

The beautiful lady only smiled at her and nodded at her grandmother.

"It's time for me to leave, my little gumdrop," Grandma Ava said.

"Leave?" Ella said, looking at the high brick walls surrounding the playground. "I don't know how you got in here, Grandma, but you'll have to get Mr. Catchings, the custodian, to unlock the gate and let you out."

Grandma Ava laughed. "The walls won't be a problem, Sweetie. I want you to say goodbye from me to all the family; can you do that for me? And please tell them all how much I love them, forever and ever."

Ella remembered feeling terribly confused. None of this was making any sense to her.

"I'm going away with my friend," Grandma Ava said. "I came to say goodbye to you because I knew that you would be able to see me."

Grandma Ava bent to kiss Ella on the forehead. "Goodbye, honey, be a good girl," she said.

Ella said that she will always remember the gentle kiss that her grandmother gave her as a token of farewell, and she will never forget watching her grandmother and the beautiful lady walk through the wall of the playground.

Later that afternoon, Ella's mother came to get her at school, and on the way home told Ella that Grandma Ava had died that morning.

"I tried to tell the family that Grandma had come by that morning at recess time with a beautiful friend to say goodbye and to tell them all how much she loved them," Ella said. "Of course, the adults believed that was how a seven-year-old child dealt with grief. Since I consistently told the same story for years afterward, I think some of the family believed me by the time I was in high school. And whether or not everyone believes me to this day, it matters not one bit to me. I know that Grandma Ava came to say goodbye to me as her angel was escorting her to Heaven."

*M*arco had been a police officer for almost two years when he was viciously attacked by a parolee on a routine enforcement stop at a convenience store.

"Although he was on parole and had been strictly ordered to stay off drugs and alcohol, I could tell that he was high the second I approached him at the store where he had been causing trouble," Marco said. "He just went wild, crazy, and he attacked me the second I approached him."

The thug smashed a liquor bottle in the officer's face.

"Somehow, I was able to stay on my feet," Marco said. "I dragged the man outside and fell against a wall, but I managed to keep my balance. My face was cut up from the broken bottle, and I was bleeding profusely from my right eye."

All around him, Officer Marco could hear the jeers and curses that encouraged the big parolee to stomp the policeman into the street. One of his greatest fears was that the street punks would decide to join in the fight on his opponent's side and participate in the gang killing of a cop. The hoodlum was taller and a lot heavier than Marco, and he was also a veteran street fighter—he certainly didn't need any help from the thugs who cheered him on.

Marco knew that he was getting the worst of it, and the steady flow of blood from his eye blinded him so he could not always see his attacker.

"I would take a punch and swing in the direction that the blow had come from," Marco said. "I was determined to keep on fighting, regardless of the odds against me."

Marco had heard a weather report on the squad-car radio as he had driven to pick up the parolee: It was 106 degrees that day. He had planned to give the man a stern talking to about his public behavior in as little time as possible, then get back into his air-conditioned vehicle. Now, it seemed that he had been fighting the big man, who was crazed by drugs and alcohol, in the heat of a blast furnace for an hour or more.

Marco had taken one vicious punch after another, and he felt that he was losing. Unable to see his opponent, he grabbed him and tried to hold him close so he could not launch his punches with such power.

"That was when I heard the voice inside my head telling me to ask God and my guardian angel for help," Marco said. "Everything had happened so fast, I had not even had time to pray for God's help. With all my soul, I asked God to let me end this terrible fight and to let me go home to my wife and little son."

Marco had seen that friends of the thug had prevented the convenience-store employee from calling the police to bring him assistance, but now, out of his one good eye, he saw a big man walk up to the patrol car and shout into the radio that an officer was down and needed immediate help. Whoever this brave man was, he was not intimidated by the neighborhood punks who were rooting for the parolee.

Knowing that help was on the way seemed to supercharge Marco's strength. "I seemed to draw from a reservoir of power that had been hidden deep inside me," he said. "I kept whaling away at the guy, and when I heard the sirens coming, I knew that I could outlast him until help arrived."

Later, Marco learned that the fight had lasted for over fifteen minutes in that awful 106-degree heat. Backup officers put the cuffs on the parolee, and both the thug and Marco were taken to an emergency room at the nearest hospital. Marco had suffered a concussion, and ten stitches were needed to close the gash on his forehead and eye.

"I was just grateful to God that I was able to go home to my wife and eleven-month-old son that night," Marco said. "And I was also grateful to the big guy who pushed aside the street punks to yell into my car radio that I needed help. I am certain that he was an angel, for when I tried later to find out who he was and to thank him for being a standup guy, nobody knew who he was, and most said that they had never seen him before in the neighborhood. I have never again gone out on even the most routine call without praying to God and asking my guardian angel to watch over me."

*B*rianna admitted that she was completely lost in thought as she walked up and down the supermarket aisles in June 2005.

"Our precious grandchildren were visiting from Arizona," she said. "Since my husband and I moved back to Kentucky, we are fortunate if we see them once a year. And now, together with our son and daughter-in-law, the three darlings were going to be staying with us for about two weeks."

Brianna was trying to recall all of their current dietary requirements and preferences as she pushed the cart ahead of her. Kitty, eighteen, was currently a vegetarian; Brent, sixteen, wanted to bulk up for football; Melanie, eleven, liked a particular brand of frozen pizza; Laura, their daughter-in-law, preferred yogurt with fruit; and Josh, their son, if he hadn't changed, liked to eat anything that wasn't moving.

Just as she was reaching for a plastic bag of frozen shrimp, Brianna felt someone tugging violently on her coat sleeve. She turned to face a rather stern-faced lady who was red in the face with agitation. She reminded Brianna of a strict teacher she had had in fourth grade. And, not to be on fashion patrol, but the woman's clothing seemed of that same 1940s vintage.

"Don't you pay any attention to your purse while you are shopping?" the woman asked in an accusative tone. "See that man standing over there next to the display of coffee cans?"

Brianna made eye contact with a man who became obviously startled that she had noticed him.

"He reminded me of a large rodent standing there," Brianna said. "He had squinty little eyes, and his nose almost seemed to be twitching, as if he were smelling out his next meal—or his next victim."

He didn't have a shopping cart, and appeared to have no interest in the various goods the supermarket offered. He only seemed interested in spotting ladies' purses that were left unwatched in carts while their owners roamed the aisles searching for bargains.

Brianna, who could never be accused of being shy, started to approach the man, and as she did so, she called out, "Why are you staring at me? What are you after?"

The man turned and walked quickly down the aisle. It was apparent to Brianna that he was making his getaway.

"I know the lady who alerted me to the purse snatcher was right at my elbow giving me support as I walked toward the man," Brianna said. "But when I turned to thank her for the heads-up, she was gone. I mean she had disappeared; she was nowhere to be seen."

Even though Brianna kept an eye out for the woman who had sounded the alarm as she shopped, she never caught another glimpse of her. As Brianna looked up one aisle and down another, it seemed that the stern-faced female vigilante had simply vanished.

"I am convinced that she was my guardian angel, alerting me to that purse predator who was roaming the supermarket that afternoon," Brianna said. "I've always believed in that old saying that we often meet angels unawares."

*F*or several weeks, Brooke said, she had been haunted by a terrible feeling that something awful was about to happen to her. Even her dreams had been troubled by a strange kind of uneasiness, a dreadful premonition of something frightful about to occur.

"I like to think that I have always tried to be a good person," Brooke told us. "I have attended church regularly since I was a small child, and I have always felt a deep love for Jesus."

One night, Brooke had a vivid dream of seeing Jesus on the cross during his crucifixion.

"There were angels ministering to him while he suffered," she said. "They comforted him by singing a beautiful song. The words and the music were so powerful and so compelling, that I woke up singing the marvelous song of the angels. I could recall the melody perfectly, but the words eluded me. There was one particularly lovely line about how they, the angels, were always near and how they sought always to protect us."

Brooke sang the song for her husband, Daniel, and their three children before they left for work and school that morning. It had seemed so familiar to Brooke, but she couldn't remember the name of the hymn. She asked them to help her recall the name of the song. They all agreed that the melody was lovely, but they all said that they were certain that they had never heard it before.

"Everyone has had that experience when you just can't remember the name of a song," Brooke said. "It almost comes to you . . . and then you lose it."

It bothered her so much that afternoon that Brooke drove over to her pastor's office in the church and sang it for him and his secretary. Since the song was definitely about angels, she thought that the two of them might be familiar with it.

Pastor Martinson and Mrs. Gaard agreed that the song sounded familiar, but they couldn't quite recall the name, or even where they had heard it before Brooke had sung it for them. The Pastor said that the melody reminded him of a Swedish folksong about angels that he had heard his grandmother sing when he was a very small boy.

One night, about a week after Brooke's mysterious dream of the "angel song," as her children termed it, she was sitting up reading a book, waiting for Daniel to get home. It was very late, and the children had been asleep for hours.

As she got up to get herself a fresh cup of coffee, Brooke was startled by the appearance of a large angel standing in the doorway of the kitchen. The angel opened his mouth and the same lovely song that Brooke had heard in her dream issued forth in waves of sound that seemed to penetrate her entire body.

"I don't know long the angel sang this enchanting, mesmerizing song," Brooke said, "but when he stopped, he told me to sit down at the dining room table. He would stay with me until Daniel returned home."

With those words, Brooke said, her consciousness went blank.

"The next thing I knew, Daniel was touching my shoulder gently and asking me if I was all right," Brooke said. "I became instantly alert, and I wasn't the least bit groggy, but it was as if time had just stood still until Daniel walked in the house."

Brooke looked at her wristwatch and was amazed to see that about three hours had passed since the angel had told her to sit down and assured her that he would stay with her until Daniel returned.

"Where's the angel?" she wondered. "He was standing there in the kitchen doorway, like he was blocking me from going in there."

Brooke was startled by a soft knocking at the front door. Daniel opened the door to two policemen, and asked them to come in.

"As Daniel had pulled into the driveway, his headlights had caught a shadowy figure looking in our kitchen window," Brooke said. "Daniel had chased the man away, but he had still called the police to check things out and to get any kind of statement from me that I might be able to give them."

Brooke could provide nothing of value for any kind of criminal investigation, for, as she told the officers, she must have fallen asleep while sitting at the dining room table, and she didn't awaken until her husband had arrived home.

The police told Brooke and Daniel that there were numerous cigarette butts beneath the kitchen window; the man had to have stood there looking into the house for quite some time.

"The officers told us that I had been very fortunate that the thug hadn't decided to come in, especially since they discovered that I had not locked the kitchen door," Brooke said. "The policemen were puzzled just what it could have been that kept the potential intruder from coming in. After all, there was only one small, 108-pound woman there to stop him. Something had kept him out."

Without hesitation, Brooke declared that it was the presence of her guardian angel that had kept the monster from invading their home and harming her or the children.

As he was leaving, one of the officers asked Brooke jokingly where he could sign up for one of those guardian angels.

"You don't have to sign up for a guardian angel, officer," she told him. "You already have one."

*W*e have all heard the expression "pennies from Heaven"; perhaps we've even sung along with the familiar tune, first introduced by Bing Crosby in the 1936 motion picture *Pennies from Heaven*. As strange as it may seem, some people claim that angels from Heaven have showered them with pennies, nickels, quarters, and even dollar bills when they needed the money most.

In the case of Mary, an unwed mother of an eleven-month-old son who had fallen on very hard times, the needed money materialized when she had only $20 left to her name. The small sum would cover diapers and baby formula, but was not enough to buy the food that she and her son needed to survive.

On a very cold, damp, windy night, Mary got out of her car in the grocery store parking lot and placed her son in a shopping cart. No one else was in sight.

"Then," she said, "three twenty-dollar bills blew up to me. Then the wind suddenly stopped. I looked right and left . . . there was no one else in the parking lot. I knew that God saw and heard my plight and sent money from Heaven."

In the fall of 1992, thirty-year-old Cindy was moving to the Toronto, Ontario, area. A cousin had promised to help her find a job good enough to support herself and her two children. Dwight, her husband of eight years, had been killed in an automobile accident, and his meager insurance policies had only covered the expenses of his burial.

Cindy was down to her last few dollars. She couldn't find the kind of job in Edmonton, Alberta, that would allow her to support her children and still have enough money to get a decent apartment in a good neighborhood. It seemed that she was given an opportunity for a second chance when her cousin Charlene called from Toronto and said that she was certain that she could find a good job for Cindy if she could manage to get there. Cindy decided to gamble the last bit of cash that she had on a bus trip to Toronto.

Cindy packed some peanut butter sandwiches and a bag of potato chips, but the food did not last the three of them very long. Her daughter Marjorie was only six and Mindy was just four, and Cindy couldn't stand it when they cried because they were hungry.

"I also knew that they would probably develop motion sickness a lot faster if their stomachs were empty, but what could I do?" Cindy asked. "It seemed like we had barely started the long bus ride when our food was gone."

Cindy promised the girls that she would get them something good to eat when they got to Winnipeg, but she knew that she was down to her last three dollars. She did not know how they could last all the way to Toronto.

Cindy finally got the girls to sleep after they shared the last peanut butter sandwich three ways. Cindy only took a small bite, and she let Marjorie and Mindy finish the small bag of potato chips.

There were only a few passengers on board at that point in the trip, but Cindy figured the bus would fill up after the Winnipeg stop. She never begged for anything in her life, but she thought that an elderly man sitting toward the back of the bus looked kind. She sat quietly for several minutes trying to get up the courage to ask him for just a few dollars for the children.

Before she got to her feet to make the humiliating trip to the back of the bus, Cindy began to pray. She asked God to have mercy on them. She asked that the elderly man would be touched by their plight and give her enough money to buy the girls a decent meal at the next restaurant where the bus stopped. Cindy knew that her cousin would lend her some money when they got to Toronto, but she had been too ashamed to admit that she had only enough money to buy the bus tickets and barely a penny more. Cindy told God that she had to have some money, or Marjorie and Mindy would be starved and sick long before they reached their final destination.

By the time she'd finished praying, Cindy was crying. That's when she felt someone touch her on the shoulder.

Cindy turned around to see a beautiful lady all dressed in white. At first, her whole body seemed to be outlined with a thin, bright illumination. Then the light kept growing, until the lady was completely enveloped in a magnificent circle of radiance. Cindy found herself believing that they were somewhere on a cloud high in the sky, rather than on a bus.

The beautiful lady told Cindy not to worry. She proclaimed that her life was going to be much better than it had ever been.

"You and the girls are going to be just fine," the radiant angel figure stated. "Know that God is good, and that we angels keep watch over you always."

With these words, the angel disappeared. But Cindy had tangible proof that the angel had visited her—a crisp new $50 bill was sticking out of her jacket pocket.

Cindy saw that the bus driver was watching her curiously in the rearview mirror. She wondered if he had seen the angel appear.

"Are you all right back there?" he asked. He could easily see that the other passengers were sleeping or sitting quietly in their seats, but here was a young mother jumping around in the aisle.

Cindy felt compelled to ask the driver if he had seen the beautiful lady who had appeared behind her.

The driver shook his head and chuckled. "No, I surely did not see such an unpaid passenger," he said. "But I noticed earlier that you seemed troubled by something. Maybe you just need a good meal. We'll be stopping soon to eat at a very good restaurant."

And now she would be able to buy Marjorie and Mindy some nourishing food. They had been living on peanut butter sandwiches and potato chips even before the trip had begun.

"I was troubled, sir, and thank you for your concern," Cindy said. "But I feel much better now that I know the angels care for me and are looking out for me and my girls."

The woman who had been sleeping a few seats away from Cindy yawned and expressed hope that some angels would check in on her pretty soon.

"You just have to remember to ask," Cindy told her, clutching the $50 of Heaven-sent help in her hand. When the bus pulled into Winnipeg, she would be able to buy the girls a nice warm meal. The rest of the trip to Toronto would seem a lot shorter with food in their stomachs. They had been provided for by an angel, and Cindy had a strong feeling that the wonderful guidance had only just begun.

Janice, a single mom, was struggling to complete college while raising her small daughter. Although money was extremely tight, Janice kept finding dimes that would materialize out of the air in the bathroom of her tiny one-bedroom apartment.

Throughout the eighteen months that she and her daughter lived in the apartment, enough dimes came out of the ether to help them get by financially. She said that at all hours of the day or night, she would "hear the distinct sound of coins dropping" in the bathroom. "Sometimes there would be several, always in the same place near the tub."

It so pleased her, she said, to believe that the falling dimes were "a sign of caring from loving beings."

"Sometimes I wondered, why dimes?" Janice admitted. "When money was really tight, I would think to myself, 'Okay, Blessed Ones, some dollar bills would be nice.' But then I thought that maybe to receive that which is truly necessary and no more was a very good teaching from the angels."

Michael has never forgotten the time that an angel brought his mother the money to pay an overdue bill.

From her birth, his baby sister Kathleen had suffered a chronic illness, which the doctor said she would one day outgrow—if they could just keep her alive long enough. Michael recalled that her bronchial tubes would spasm in such a way that the child could inhale, but she could not exhale unless someone gave her artificial respiration.

It seemed that poor little Kathleen was forever in and out of hospitals and clinics, and when she was home, the doctor had to visit no less than three times a week.

Although Michael loved his sister, there were times when he knew that the family had just enough money to scrape by and not a penny extra; and he was aware that Kathleen's medical expenses ate the family budget, leaving barely enough to keep the family going. Michael's father worked two jobs and did his best to provide; his mother couldn't go back to her old job because Kathleen needed constant care.

Michael was about seven, and Kathleen was three or so, when the angel miracle occurred. Although the rent was due on this particular day, their mother had spent a good portion of the money set aside for Mr. Bumble, as Michael's father called him, on heavy woolen snowsuits to keep the cold winter away from Kathleen and Michael.

As Michael recalled, the shortage was only around $30, but it was a lot of money for a working-class family to come up with in an afternoon. He knew that his mother had made a novena to the Blessed Virgin, praying that somehow she could convince Mr. Bumble to grant them another week or so to come up with the rent.

And then the little miracle occurred. His mother was putting something away in the kitchen cabinet when an envelope fell out and fluttered to the floor. Puzzled, she picked up the envelope and opened it. She let out a small scream that startled Michael and awakened the napping Kathleen. Inside the envelope were three $10 bills. She now had just enough to pay Mr. Bumble his rent money and not a penny more.

Michael said that his parents were firmly convinced that the Blessed Virgin had heard Mother's prayers, and sent an angel to deliver desperately needed money. It was certain that neither of his parents had put the money in the kitchen cabinet for safekeeping and then forgotten about it. Money was far too scarce in the household to have misplaced a single cent, to say nothing of $30.

Michael's father always thought it was meaningful that the envelope was marked "Airmail"; this was proof that it had come from on high, from the angels.

Helen had reached such a financially desperate time in her life that she didn't have enough money for her three sons' lunch the next day at school. Although she only needed $3, she was so embarrassed by her complete lack of funds that she decided to keep the boys home from school. Her twelve-year-old son, who had perfect attendance, protested and said that he absolutely could not miss school the next day, lunch money or not.

There was a strange noise from the kitchen, and when Helen and her older son investigated, they saw some quarters scattered on the floor.

In her account, Helen admitted that she was frightened and wanted to run out of the house. However, her son entered the kitchen, picked up the quarters, and placed them on the table, declaring them to be icy cold. There was exactly $3 in quarters.

"They're from Grandma," her son said, referring to Helen's deceased mother. "She always gave me quarters."

Even better than providing enough money for her sons' lunch money the next day, Helen concluded, was the good news that the quarters from Grandma and the angels in Heaven signified that things were going to get better for the family. Life just seemed to come together for them that night, and they never had to go without again.

*I*n February 2007, Lucille received a telephone call from her brother Owen, giving her the bad news that their mother was very sick and had been hospitalized. According to the information that Owen had received, her physician had placed her on a ventilator to help her breathe, and had advised Owen that things did not look good. If her children wanted to see her before she died, they needed to get there as soon as possible.

Lucille said that she prayed hard to God that she would be able to get there before anything happened. Although Owen lived only an hour or so from the hospital, Lucille had an eight-hour drive ahead of her.

By the time Lucille arrived at the hospital, her mother was off the ventilator. "She cried when I walked into the room," Lucille said. "I told Owen that I would sit with Mom for a few hours while he took a break."

As Lucille sat there beside the hospital bed reading a magazine, trying to be quiet so her mother could rest, she was startled out of her reverie when her mother began to sing.

"I thought Mom was sleeping," Lucille said. "And then she started to sing this song. And boy, did she ever sing it! The notes came out loud and clear as church bells on a frosty morning."

Lucille is in her mid-fifties, and she has always been a great music lover. Whether someone plays a hymn, rhythm and blues, or country rock, she said it would be difficult to stump her.

"But this was a song that I had never heard in my entire lifetime," she said, "and it was the most beautiful song I have ever heard."

Within a few minutes, every nurse and candy striper on the floor was crowding into the hospital room to hear the lovely song that was echoing down the hallways.

"Mom had the biggest smile on her face while she sang," Lucille said. "When she stopped, she fell back asleep. A few minutes later, when she awakened, I asked her where she had ever heard such a beautiful song. Mom didn't know what I was talking about. She didn't remember singing any song at all."

Later, when Owen returned from getting some dinner and a brief nap, he was puzzled by so many nurses complimenting him on his mother's beautiful singing of a song that none of them had ever heard. Was his mother a song writer?

What, Owen asked Lucille, had happened while he had been away? He couldn't remember their mother ever singing, other than hymns with the rest of the congregation in church.

Lucille tried her best to recall some of the words and the melody for her brother, but she hardly felt equal to the example set by their mother.

"I told Owen that I would never forget the beauty of that song," Lucille said. "And since we both agreed that Mom had never been a singer, I told him that I believed that song had come from an angel, an angel who had used the power of the voice to heal Mom."

Their mother did improve, and she was released from the hospital into the care of a nursing home.

"Mom lived for six more months," Lucille said, "then passed quietly in her sleep. The time that the angels had granted her was important, and she was able to get her affairs in order and to spend some precious time with dear relatives and friends."

A few weeks after her mother went home to God, Lucille said, she came down with a terrible cough and a very high fever. After three visits with her family doctor, she still lay all night coughing, unable to sleep. No medicine seemed to touch the tightness and congestion in her chest. It seemed inevitable that she was going to have to be taken to the hospital.

"One night, I was so miserable that I thought I was going to have to call an ambulance," Lucille said. "Then, between fits of coughing, I heard this lovely voice singing the same beautiful song that had issued from our mother's mouth when she was in the hospital. Since I knew the song wasn't coming from my mouth, I got up to look around to see if I could find the source of this heavenly music."

Lucille checked her apartment to see if a radio, television set, or CD player had been left on. "I really knew that I wouldn't find any such logical explanation, because no one on Earth can sing like that or make music like the song that I heard that night at Mom's hospital bed and now in my own home."

Lucille went back to her bedroom and lay back down. "I just decided to enjoy the beautiful music and see what would happen," she said.

As she lay quietly listening to the heavenly music, her body began to relax and she fell asleep, enjoying the first full rest she had had for many nights. When she awoke, she was no longer coughing. She felt renewed in body, mind, and spirit.

"The cough did not return," Lucille said. "The angel song had healed me while I slept. I know that I heard Mom's voice among those heavenly singers. I know that she is at peace and that someday I will stand beside her in that joyous angel choir."

*B*ernadette Bay O'Shaughnessy, author of the time-travel romance *The Letters from Inverness Terrace*, had a boyfriend from Texas who had told her of an incident where an angel saved his life.

Lenny was a machinist, and one time he was in a driving rainstorm in Louisiana. As he was cautiously maneuvering the slippery roads, a woman in white popped up right in front of him.

He thought that he had run over her, because as he stepped on his brakes, his pickup came to a screeching halt, and she disappeared.

He stopped and got out to see if he had hurt her (or God forbid, killed her). Well, he looked around on all sides, even under the truck, and found nothing; not even a dead armadillo.

Lenny continued on, driving at a crawl, just in case anyone else popped up. And guess what happened? A bridge that he always crossed had been washed out!

If Lenny had continued at the speed he had been driving, he would have gone off into the river and drowned.

So was this "lady" in white that had run out into the road in that storm a guiding angel? Sounds like one.

Bernadette told us of another occasion, on a Christmas Eve several years ago. Her husband and she were driving one of their older cars—a 1980 Buick Skylark—on her way home from work

"Our engine stalled out, and we had no idea how we would get home, as it was late at night," she said. "But then, out of nowhere, a huge white pickup arrived with a nice man who pulled us to our driveway! We thanked him, went inside, and when I went to wave to him to let him know we were all right, he had just disappeared into thin air!

"Awhile later I was listening to a lady disk jockey who plays nighttime romantic music, and she played the record 'Angels Among Us.' I thought it was very appropriate."

$\mathcal{M}$adeline had just picked up her sister Lily from an overnight stay in a Lincoln, Nebraska, hospital. Both women lived in a small prairie town about a two-hour drive from the larger city, and their family doctor had ordered some tests for Lily that couldn't be adequately performed in the local clinic. Madeline left home at 7:30 A.M. on a bright, sunny winter day in mid-December 2003. By the time they had checked Lily out of the hospital, the ominous dark clouds that had gathered in the northwest told them that a winter's storm was liable to hit very soon.

Madeline was eager to leave the constraints of big-city driving as quickly as possible and hit the open road. The drive home would take them across stretches of nothing but range country, where shelter and help would be few and far between.

"Let me drive," Lily said. "I'm faster and better than you are behind the wheel. We've got to beat this storm; we don't want to get stranded out in the open somewhere."

Madeline conceded that Lily might be a faster driver, but she argued that Lily had also accumulated quite a few speeding citations. They wouldn't get home any sooner if a Highway Patrolman pulled them over and gave them a ticket.

Lily grumbled that she didn't want to spend another night away from her babies.

Madeline reminded her sister that their mother was looking after both of their children.

"That's what I mean," Lily said. "She'll have those two little dickens's of mine spoiled with cookies and chocolate bars."

It started snowing twenty minutes out of Lincoln. Light flurries at first, that swirled crazily in the wind.

Another ten minutes and the snow was coming down heavily, driven by a thirty-mile-an-hour wind that caused white-out conditions and zero visibility.

"I can't see," Madeline said. "I'll have to pull over."

"Keep going," Lily insisted. "You'll slide down in the ditch."

"If I keep going, I might hit some slower-moving car ahead of us," Madeline said. "I'm pulling over. I can't see. The snow is coming too fast for the wipers to handle."

Lily slumped forward, clutching her stomach. She told Madeline that she was feeling nauseated from all the tests. She wanted to get home.

Madeline put her arm around her sister's shoulder and assured her that after the white-out passed, they would be able to get on their way again. The wind was bound to slacken its fury, and the windshield wipers would be able to do a better job of creating a peephole for her to see the road through.

"Yeah," Lily agreed sarcastically. "The storm should easily let up in a couple of days."

"Okay," Madeline said. "You're right. We have to keep moving or we'll become a snow bank."

It was when she shifted into drive that Madeline discovered that although Lily's fear that they would slide into the ditch had not been realized, one of the rear wheels had become anchored behind the ridge of the concrete road and would not budge.

"Give her some gas; gun it and break free of the ice," Lily shouted when she heard the wheels spinning.

Madeline explained that it wasn't a patch of ice that held them fast; they were stuck in some kind of rut. They could spin and squeal the tires until they melted, but that wouldn't get them free.

Madeline said that she was going to call for help on her cell phone. After a futile search through her purse, she had a flash of memory: She had left the phone on the kitchen counter that morning while she put on her three-year-old daughter's snowsuit. She had become distracted and had forgotten to pick up the phone and place it in her purse.

Lily scowled at her sister, then retrieved her own phone from her purse. It was dead. She had used it too often in the hospital without recharging it.

They hadn't seen another vehicle since they had pulled off the highway twenty minutes ago.

"I hope you have some blankets and chow in this vehicle," Lily sighed, "because we are likely to be here until the spring thaw."

Even as Lily made her dire prediction, Madeline saw headlights approaching through the heavy snow.

"Whoever that is, he is going to stop and help us get back on the highway so we can get out of here," Madeline said as she opened the door on the driver's side.

Becoming uncharacteristically bold, Madeline stepped out a few feet onto the highway and began to wave her hands frantically. The man driving the car clearly saw her, but he chose to drive on without stopping. He made a gesture with his hands that he dare not stop for fear he himself would get stuck in the snow that was banking across the highway.

Frustrated, nearly soaked to the skin, and feeling more than a little desperate, Madeline got back in the car and turned up the heater. At least they had the warmth and shelter of the car. But then she noticed that the gas gauge was much lower than she had thought.

"Lily's teeth were chattering," Madeline said. "I could see that she was left far weaker from the tests than she had let on. I pulled a blanket from the backseat and pulled it over her. Lily huddled under the blanket, then smiled up at me and said, 'I think it is time for some amazing grace.'"

Ever since they had been young girls and had attended a religious revival meeting with their grandmother, the two sisters had spoken of 'time for amazing grace' whenever they were in any kind of trouble. It had become their code phrase for praying like all get out because they needed some heavenly helpers. Madeline and Lily clasped hands and prayed for someone to come help them.

Madeline shut off the car to conserve gas. The wind had picked up, the temperature had dropped, and the snow was getting heavier. It was getting very cold in the car, when Madeline saw headlights illuminating her frosted rearview mirror. Within moments, she could see the lights of a tow truck pulling off the highway directly behind them.

A handsome man in a garage mechanic's jumpsuit tapped on her side window and told her that he would have them free in just a few minutes. He attached a chain to the front of their car and pulled them free.

"One of the first things I noticed about him, other than how handsome he was, was that he didn't wear a coat or a cap," Madeline said. "He just had on that jump-suit, like he was working in a heated garage, not standing out in the open in the midst of a raging blizzard."

After he had freed their vehicle, the man told them to keep driving ahead, carefully and cautiously.

"I don't know if you've had your radio on, but the storm isn't as wide in scope as it appears right here in this area," he told them. "The wind lessens about three miles ahead, and the snow is not nearly as heavy. You should have pretty comfortable driving in about eight miles and very good driving conditions on the rest of your way home."

The positive weather forecast coming from the confident mechanic did a great deal to brighten the sisters' spirits.

Madeline reached for her purse and asked the man how much they owed him for pulling them off the hang up on the shoulder.

"He smiled, just as at ease as you please, standing out in the freezing cold of a winter storm as if it were a sunny summer's day, and told me that there was no charge," Madeline said. "He saw that we were in trouble, and he just wanted to help us."

Madeline insisted and handed him a $50 bill. "Take it," she said. "It's small enough payment for what you did. We were in deep trouble until you came along."

Madeline remembered that he looked at the bill in a strange way, as if she had handed him some mysterious artifact. Then he handed it back to her and told her to buy something extra for Christmas for her kids.

Just as he was about to step up into his tow truck, he turned and shouted over the wind, "Merry Christmas, Madeline! Merry Christmas, Lily!"

Madeline swears that neither of them told the stranger their names, nor did he ever see any driver's licenses or any kind of identification.

"But he knew our names," Madeline said. "And if that wasn't enough to prove to us that our hero was an angel come in answer to our prayers, as he drove away we could hear him singing 'Amazing Grace' in a very robust baritone."

*V*irginia, a retired schoolteacher, wrote to tell of her strange experience on a late November day in northern Wisconsin. The sky was heavy with snow clouds, the wind had reached gale force, and it was very cold. And then, one of the tires on her old Buick blew out.

She managed to get the car off the road and onto a crossroad about ten yards ahead. Then she walked back to the highway, hoping to flag down someone who could stop at the little town she had whizzed through about five miles back and send a tow truck.

Fortunately, Virginia was wearing her old army field coat with the liner, but it was getting darker and colder, and she was steadily feeling more helpless. No one would stop to help her, and she didn't know what to do.

Then a voice in her head said, "You'd better pray," so she did.

Within about three minutes, a Model T Ford without a top drove up and stopped. She described the three people in the antique car as "unbelievable." The driver had a beard and wore blue jeans, a denim jacket, and an old brown fedora. The young man in the back seat was dressed exactly as the old man, and was lounging with one foot on the back of the front seat, a silly grin on his freckled face. His carefree attitude suggested that he thought he was riding in a Rolls Royce. The woman who was seated beside the driver wore only a light cotton housedress and a tattered brown shawl against the terrible cold.

"I couldn't understand how she could keep from shivering in the freezing wind," Virginia said. "In fact, all three of them acted as though they thought it was the middle of the summer."

The bizarre trio offered to give Virginia a ride to a service station, but she thanked them and explained that she didn't want to leave her car. The bearded man repeated his invitation, and the woman urged Virginia to get in the car and go with them.

When Virginia once again graciously refused their offer, they seemed very reluctant to leave without her, but they finally accepted her decision and began to edge the Model T back into traffic.

Virginia remembers that once the antique car got back into traffic, it appeared to take off at over sixty miles an hour. "I stood there gazing after the strange trio, not believing what had just happened," she said. "Again that voice in my head said, 'You have been talking to angels.' Then, in the blinking of an eye, the Model T and its strange passengers, had disappeared from sight."

Virginia had no more than a few minutes to deal with her remarkable encounter with the mysterious motorists when a wrecker pulled off the highway and parked in front of her car. Without a word to Virginia, the man got out of the truck and began to work on the flat tire.

She asked him how long he had lived in the area, and if he happened to know the people who drove the Model T, but he didn't answer her. She went on to describe the occupants of the old car, and how inappropriately they had been dressed against the bitter wind and cold, but the service attendant seemed unable to hear her—or at least he gave no sign that he did.

"When he finished, I asked him how much I owed him," Virginia said. "He looked at me strangely, as if he had no idea what I was talking about. I finally handed him a ten-dollar bill and told him to take it to his boss. He accepted the bill hesitantly, looking at it as if I had presented him with a great mystery. Finally he nodded, as if understanding the exchange at last, and said, 'Oh, all right.' With those few words, I found out that he did possess the ability to speak. He got back into the wrecker, and with a wave of his hand—the first sign he had shown of friendliness—he drove away.

"It has now been many years since that strange experience," Virginia said, concluding her encounter with the unknown, "and I have often wondered if I had got into that old Model T with its mysterious passengers, would I, too, have disappeared along with them?

"If the out-of-place, inappropriately dressed entities were angels, then I have decided that the truck driver who fixed my tire was also an angel. He couldn't have been sent to me by the first angels in the Model T, because he couldn't have arrived on the scene so quickly. And that was probably why he didn't seem to know what I was talking about as I described the other three beings; he had been sent to help me by some other heavenly dispatcher."

*L*ogan ran out of gas while crossing Kansas in the midst of a blizzard.

"I'm always nagging my wife to watch the fuel gauge, because she's run out of gas two or three times within a few blocks of our home," Logan said. "But here am I, in the midst of a prairie blizzard, underestimating the time it would take to get from one town to another, and out of gas. I couldn't even run the car to keep me warm."

As closely as he could figure, it was a five-mile walk to the nearest turnoff where he could buy gasoline. Since this was the loneliest stretch of highway on his sales route, he would be unlikely to be able to get a ride with a truck driver or anyone willing to stop in the blizzard and pick him up. Because he was a fairly fast walker, Logan figured that if he wasn't able to get a ride, it would take him about two hours to get to the turnoff, and two hours to get back.

However, Logan calculated that particular time scenario based on a fine summer/spring/fall day, not in the midst of a blizzard. Besides, he wasn't dressed for such an ordeal; he wore dress shoes, a three-piece suit, and a lightweight coat. The way the wind was howling outside his vehicle, he estimated the wind chill to be about ten degrees above freezing, and with the amount of heavy snow that was falling, he would be blinded by the combination of snow and wind and wander off the highway.

"I had really only been stalled on the shoulder of the road just long enough to begin to get really cold and really worried, when a pickup appeared out of nowhere," Logan said. "I gave a loud prayer of thanks when I saw that the pickup had the name of a service station from the next town on the map."

The pickup pulled up in front of Logan's vehicle, and an attractive young woman in coveralls got out of the cab. Logan remembers clearly that she wore a baseball cap over her long blonde hair, and that she wore no coat over her coveralls. In her right hand, she carried a plastic five-gallon container of gasoline.

"There are only a couple of gallons left," she told Logan, who had got out of his vehicle to receive the container. "They'll get you to the gas station at the exit."

Logan poured the gasoline, careful not to spill a drop. When he glanced up from the gas cap, his rescuer was already getting back in her pickup.

"Just pay Dusty at the station," she said over her shoulder. "I have a busy schedule this afternoon."

And without another word, she drove off into the storm.

Within a few more minutes, Logan was filling his tank at the gas station near the highway exit. When he walked into the small, cluttered office, Logan inquired if the man tending the cash register was Dusty.

The man acknowledged that that was what folks in town called him, and he asked if the two of them had met on a previous occasion.

Logan explained that the young woman who drove Dusty's service truck had come to his rescue out on the highway and had given him a container with a few gallons of gas, enough to get him into the station.

Dusty recognized the container and pointed out his initials painted near the nozzle, but he laughed at the statement that he had a service truck and a pretty, young woman as a mechanic.

"What you see is what you get, friend," Dusty said, nodding around his small office. "Two pumps for gas, one for diesel outside, and a rack of windshield wipers and some cans of oil inside. That is my domain."

Thinking he was the butt of some countrified joke, Logan teased Dusty about having such a beautiful blonde working for him.

"In my dreams, mister, in my dreams," Dusty laughed. "If such a lovely creature rescued you from the blizzard, then she had to have been an angel."

Once Logan was convinced that the station owner had no service garage, no service truck, and no lovely blonde working for him, he drove away convinced that he had been saved by an angel.

"For those skeptics who argue that it was just a kind young woman who stopped and gave me a few gallons of gas," Logan said, "let me remind them that this service truck was plastered with decals advertising the brand of gasoline and the name of the Kansas town just ahead. And remember, that was Dusty's gas container. I know that it was an angel who heard my prayers and saw the mess that I was in. I also remember her last words to me were that she had a busy afternoon ahead of her; it stands to reason that angels are extra busy during floods, earthquakes, hurricanes, and blizzards."

*I*n the summer of 1976, Rebecca Jernigan, host of the popular radio program *Journeys with Rebecca*, was twenty-one, the mother of two small boys, in the process of a divorce, and on her own for the first time in her young life. Although many other young women have found themselves in similar circumstances, Rebecca shared with us the personal journey that brought her to a higher level of awareness and a deeper understanding of miracles, angels, and the true power of heart.

To better understand the enormity of her spiritual journey, Rebecca told us briefly what happened during her first twenty-one years to bring her to that day.

"My gifts—spirit communication, clairvoyance, clairaudience, and so forth—were made known to me when I was about four," she said. "I was trying to have a conversation with my mother, who was talking to the newest member of the family, a man who had just recently married my aunt. I remember pulling on Mother's skirt to get her attention. My mother turned to me and said 'What?' and I proceeded to say that my new uncle was a bad man."

Rebecca's horrified mother scolded her and demanded to know what on earth she was talking about—such things were not nice to say about people, especially ones you were meeting for the first time.

Little Rebecca held her ground, insisting that her new uncle was a bad man, because the man standing over there had told her so.

Rebecca was referring to the spirit guide that had always made his presence known to her, but no one else in the room saw any man but her new uncle, who did prove to be quite an unsavory character.

After the scolding, the harsh words, and the mean looks that she received that day, Rebecca quickly arrived at the realization that she was not to tell anyone about the spirits that she saw and talked to, because other people could not see them.

"Through the years, I continued with my communications with my guides," Rebecca said. "They were ever there, always giving me an indication of the events that were to unfold in my daily life growing up."

When she was fifteen, her father died. "Although there was a part of me that was really sad," Rebecca said, "the event of his death forever changed my life and the life of my mother and three older brothers. One day I woke up and realized that I no longer had to be fearful of the daily onslaught of abuse. Oh my, what a revelation."

Rebecca explained that her father was an alcoholic. "And not a very nice one, either," she said. "He abused all of us, including my mother. The abuse was a daily, ongoing cycle with him. My mother did not have the ability to cope well with emotions, so she became very distant with all of us—me more so than the rest. She knew I was 'different' and preferred to keep me away from others and herself. Because of her distancing herself from me, I became very despondent, and more and more of my time was spent in communication with my guides."

After her father's death, Rebecca's mother was no longer just distant, she was often entirely absent. "She frequently left me by myself for days at a time to get myself off to school, clean house, and all the other things that I had done so well for years," Rebecca said. "I only know that at that time I finally had some freedom—the first I ever had. So, needless to say, I went about trying to discover something, anything to take away the pain and abuse of those years."

It was not long before Rebecca met the man who would be the father of her two children. Rebecca hoped that she would be able to begin the kind of life that she had dreamed about as a child; one with love, happiness, and her spirit guides there to assist her.

Regretfully, Rebecca recalls, the honeymoon was over about two hours after she married him. "We had an argument—the first of many—and that is the day the abuse began with him," she said. "The abuse escalated, but when it involved the children, I made a promise to them and to myself that they would not have the life that I had had growing up.

"One day after an attack on my youngest child, I left. Within that same day, I found a place to live, moved, and set up for the start of what I thought would be a new life with my children.

"After only a few months he located us, and then the horror began all over again. I used to lie in bed and wonder what I had done to have this life. I must have deserved this, I thought! I must be a terrible person for these horrific things to just keep happening to me!"

The despondency that Rebecca had felt as a child was back in full force, perhaps even stronger than before.

One day, when her little ones were taking a nap, she decided to lie down as well.

"I was tired, defeated, deflated—and I did not know how to go on in this world with these overwhelming feelings that I had now been carrying for twenty-one years," she said.

It was midafternoon in the summer, and it was hot. Rebecca was on her bed, lying on her back with silent tears running down her face, trying to find some release for the emotions she was feeling.

"I remember, through my eyelids that the room seemed to be getting brighter," she said. "I opened my eyes, and I saw that coming in through the window of my room was this light—golden, white light! I closed my eyes, thinking I must be dreaming. I opened them again, and this light was coalescing at the end of my bed.

"I remember thinking, 'Strange, I do not feel fear at all; I feel at ease and comfortable.'

"This Light kept flowing in, and as I watched, it began to take form and shape. The shape became humanlike, and then it grew and stood there looking at me for a moment, a moment still suspended in my mind. The feeling was one of peace and amazement.

"Then this form spread wings—these wings were as wide as the room was—and I remember thinking, 'God has sent an angel!'

"This angel then began to move slowly over me from the foot of the bed to the top of the bed, slowly filling the entire room with this light."

As the angel and the light moved over her, Rebecca said that the sensation that she felt was one of being weightless, as if all the weight that she had been carrying for many years was being taken away.

"Once this angel got back to the foot of the bed again and the light subsided, I felt the wise presence of the character of the angel, and I knew that, indeed, this angel had come in to relieve my mind and heart of burdens that I had been carrying. I also perceived that the angel's presence would make me more understanding of others."

Rebecca has said that the beautiful angel communicated so many things to her in those few moments that it has literally taken her years to decode the massive amount of information imparted to her that day.

She watched as the angelic being folded its wings and began to reverse the process.

"As I watched it leave again," Rebecca said, "I realized that much time had passed, for the sun was much lower in the sky. In fact, several hours had passed! As I observed the process of the angel leaving, it seemed to float up into the sky and meld with the colors of the now late-afternoon sun.

"I lay there for a while longer and realized that I no longer felt despondent, that hope, faith, and love had returned to my heart. I knew that I had been given a gift, a gift that would be the strength in the years to come to raise my children and to communicate more fully with those guides and angels that had always been with me.

"I must tell you now of that communication with the angel," Rebecca concluded. "What it imparted to me was this: I had chosen this life—my parents, brothers, marriage, children, and all the other challenges up to this point and beyond. It was now known to me that the next years to come would be a stripping away of all the baggage of those negative experiences. This was a true empowering for me! I was not a victim, nor were my children. We were and are a part of a much bigger picture here—the Creator, angels, guides, and other light beings that are here to assist us in our knowledge and growth to become more than what we think we are, to the truth of who we are!

"This experience with this most beautiful presence was the beginning of a lifelong commitment to become aware, to help others, to be more understanding and compassionate, and to impart to others that which I was given all those years ago!"

*A*lone at Christmas in 2005, a very depressed twenty-six-year-old Alex rented a cabin "way off in the boonies of Wyoming to seek peace and solace.

"In retrospect," he admitted, "I think that I was really looking for a quiet place to be miserable, moody, and as disagreeable as possible. Someone had once told me that to be in the mountains was to raise the spirits with wonder at the majesty of God and Nature; but someone else had said that living at the base of mountains only made you feel small and insignificant with a terrible inferiority regarding your infinitesimal nonworth in the great scheme of things. I thought being in the shadow of the Bighorn Mountains would either elevate my spirit or crush it into scattered atoms."

The reasons for Alex's negativity lay in what he termed the "Domino Effect of Doom."

First, his boss had offered him the choice of a demotion or a pink slip. With job opportunities in the area at a dismal low, Alex accepted the demotion.

Second, the woman that he had been about to ask to marry him informed him over dinner at the elegant restaurant that he really couldn't afford that she was seeing someone else and they had become serious about one another. The diamond engagement ring in Alex's jacket pocket suddenly felt as though it weighed fifty pounds.

Third, his sister had just begun seriously dating a guy who had been Alex's nemesis all through high school. Although Alex hadn't seen the fellow for years, he could only think of him as a jerk, as someone who had risen barely a few feet from the low end of the gene pool.

As Alex neared the cabin where he would spend the next two nights, he stopped at a small country store and picked up some supplies. As he drove the narrow road that wound through thick groves of trees, he could clearly see that there were no other cabins near his.

There was plenty of tinder, sheets of newspaper, and well-seasoned logs in the fireplace, so it wasn't long before Alex had a bright and crackling fire going. The cabin was small—one bedroom, a kitchenette, and the sitting room in front of the fireplace.

Alex said that he did pick up a couple of six packs of beer at the store, but—and he stresses this is important—he only had one beer with his microwave Christmas Eve dinner that night.

"It was childhood residue from earlier, happier days," he explained. "It just didn't feel right to drown my sorrows in beer on Christmas Eve. Christmas Eve was a night that our family had greatly revered when I was a kid. We had always gone to church, then come home to hang up our stockings. Father Christmas came in the night and left gifts in front of the tree to be opened on Christmas morning."

When Alex was seventeen, his father had died in a freak boating accident at the age of thirty-eight. Two years later, his mother had married a man that she had met on a tour to Italy. As soon as Alex and his sister, who was a year and a half younger than he, had entered college, his mother and stepfather, a man Alex had never trusted and regarded as a disreputable snake-oil salesman, moved to Denver.

His sister's messages on his answering machine begging to get together at Christmas had been ignored, because she had committed the unforgivable offense of dating the supreme creep from his high school days.

So, Alex sat alone in front of the fireplace, watching each new log slowly transform into glowing embers and gray ashes. Old memories of happier days rushed over him with increasingly powerful waves of emotion.

"When I started to mist up once or twice, I knew it was time to go to bed," he said. "It was enough of nostalgia ad nauseum. It wasn't even midnight, but it had been a long drive and a pretty exhausting week, so I decided to go to bed."

Although Alex grumbled that the bedsprings must have been replaced with strands of rope, he soon fell asleep.

"I was awakened a few hours later by the sound of a magnificent choir singing in utmost earnestness and with remarkable vigor," Alex said. "I was quite disoriented, and it took me a few moments to identify my surroundings and to realize just where I was. As I blinked my way into full wakefulness, I was wholeheartedly absorbed with the mystery of just where the voices were coming from."

Alex knew there was no radio in the cabin, and the small television set near the fireplace had been ignored since his arrival.

"I opened a window and the voices became louder still," Alex said. "There were no other cabins in sight. The nearest small town was at least six miles away. There was no country church in the area."

The more Alex listened, the more he became convinced that he was not hearing any earthly choir. The powerful, emotionally moving voices were not singing any Christmas carols that he recognized, though he said that the music had a kind of Christmas feeling to it. Some verses that he would begin to think sounded familiar would suddenly soar off into new heights of beautiful, but totally unfamiliar, celestial sounds.

"I guess the description of the music that most readily comes to mind is 'joyous,'" Alex said. "It was as if some incredibly talented and gifted choir was celebrating the birth of new beginnings and new life. It was as if I was hearing what those shepherds once heard while tending their flocks so long ago; a declaration of peace on Earth and of blessings to all those of good will."

Alex doesn't know how long he listened to the music. It might have been minutes or hours, but the exultation that he experienced caused him to examine his own life and assess his own failings as a person of goodwill.

"Ever since Dad had been killed, I had been angry at the world," Alex said. "I had not been a person of joy, peace, or goodwill toward anyone, even my own family. I had been quick to find fault and very slow to forgive or to forget."

The angels that Alex had heard on high that Christmas Eve transformed his life. He was filled with a new, positive attitude and a resolution to re-enter the world as a person of goodwill to all. The very next morning, he was on his cell phone, proclaiming a merry Christmas to his mother, stepfather, and sister.

"I even agreed to meet Sis and her boyfriend for dinner when I got back in town," Alex said, "and in the summer of 2006, I was best man at their wedding."

Alex went on to add that he returned to his job with a new attitude and an unquenchable ambition, and soon no longer had to worry about getting a pink slip. He was, in fact, promoted. His love life took a turn for the better as well: Alex found a woman that he is pleased to call his soul mate.

*N*ina's father had been extremely upset when he learned that she had taken a job at a restaurant that required her to dress in a costume that he did not deem dignified or suitable for a young lady to wear in a public place.

"He told me that he should clamp me in leg irons," Nina said, "but then he lightened up and said that he was just worried about me working in such an atmosphere. I explained that the place was not at all like some of the other restaurants that catered primarily to guys. The restaurant where I worked had a country theme, and we waitresses were required to dress like milk maids—practically Victorian compared to other places. And besides, we needed the money."

Nina was nineteen and working hard to fulfill both her parents' and her own dream of becoming an elementary school teacher. Her mother and father already had full-time jobs, and her brother was handicapped. Although he was a good-natured child who had never complained, his special needs did place a steady financial drain on the family's bank account.

When Nina first started working at the restaurant, either her father or mother would try to pick her up after work. Whenever Nina was on the late shift, however, she would take a taxi home.

One night, her father returned from a part-time job and learned she would be working particularly late that night. He frowned when he learned how late she would be coming home, and beckoning her to come nearer, he removed the St. Christopher medal from around his neck and placed it around Nina's, "to protect her."

Nina smiled at the gesture, but couldn't resist teasing her father. "I thought St. Christopher was the patron saint of travelers," she said. She knew that her father had once been a devout Catholic, but in recent years, the family usually attended services only on Christmas and Easter Sunday. Nina had never even received her first communion.

Placing an arm around her shoulders and giving her a warm hug, her father informed her that St. Christopher was said by some to have been a giant of a fellow who would sometimes carry people across rivers on his shoulders. "He'll look after you, Honey," he told her.

That night was the first time since she had started work at the restaurant that they experienced a rowdy crowd. Nina remembers that the patrons were mostly men attending a convention in town. Due to their rude behavior, she didn't bother to make small talk and learn who they were or whom they represented.

Nina's shift ended at three o'clock, and she hoped that she would have enough energy and patience to hold out until then. Last call for bar drinks came at two, but by then most of the raucous crowd was feeling no pain and suffering no regrets for their crude comments and actions.

Nina called for a cab and went to get her coat.

As she walked to the front door of the restaurant, one of the bus boys told her that she had better wait inside for her cab, but Nina said she had to get some fresh air. The smell of tobacco smoke, beer, and spilled cocktails had become too much for her to take another minute.

It was a cool night, and she took a deep breath the moment she stepped outside. She had applied for an office job; it wouldn't be quite as much money, and there would be no tips, but the working conditions on a galley ship would be preferable to working such disgusting crowds as she had that night.

It took a few minutes for her to notice that two men had come out of the restaurant to position themselves on either side of her.

Nina recognized them at once. "Two of the loudest, most offensive creeps who had been making suggestive comments to me all night long," she said. "I had seen them leave a couple hours ago. Now they decided to come back even more liquored up than when they left, and they had decided to become much more aggressive than simply making crude and flirtatious remarks to me."

One of them said something, slurring his words drunkenly, and then both of them were trying to pull her toward a car they had waiting in the alley next to the restaurant. Nina tried to scream, but a rough hand was clamped over her mouth.

Nina fought as best she could, but the two men were strong and determined, and their sense of right and wrong had been drowned in too many glasses of alcohol.

"One of them opened the car door, got in, and began to pull me by the shoulders while the other man was trying to lift me up by the feet and push me in," Nina said. "That was when this big guy all dressed in ragged clothing seemed to rise up right out of the trash cans and rubbish in the alley. With one blow, he knocked the guy trying to lift my feet completely flat."

When the other man got out of the car and came running around to jump their attacker, Nina said that her rescuer picked him up as if he were a child and threw him into the trash cans. The man moaned and seemed in no hurry to get back up and return to the fight.

At that moment, the cab pulled up and honked twice. Nina knew that the cabbie wouldn't wait around if she weren't there, especially if he could see that there was a fight going on in the alley.

"I ran to the cab, knocked on the window, and told him I was there, don't leave me," Nina said. "I reached into my purse. I had received well over a hundred dollars in tips that night. I wanted to give it all to the ragged homeless man for coming to my rescue. No exaggeration, he could well have saved my life."

But when Nina turned to reward her savior from the streets, she saw only her two attackers lying in the alley. Her big hero in the tattered clothes had disappeared.

The cabbie beeped his horn and told her to hurry and get in. When she explained that she wanted to reward the big man who saved her from the two brutes who had attacked her, the driver frowned his impatience and told her that when he drove up, his headlights had only spotlighted her running away from the two drunken bums sprawled in the alley. There was no big guy, no other person around.

When Nina told her parents what had happened that night, her father declared her rescue to have been the intervention of St. Christopher.

Nina said that she believed that it was her guardian angel—who could certainly deliver a mean knockout punch.

The only explanation Frank had for a strange experience that happened to him when he was struggling to establish his business was that an angel had chosen to intervene on his behalf.

Back in 1987, Frank was working nearly around the clock to make a success of his antique shop. "As the old saying goes, I had been down so long that the bottom looked like up to me," Frank recalls.

Frank had married Hailey, his high school sweetheart, four months after they graduated in 1980, and they had two children, Jack and Janice, in just a little over three years. By the time Jack was in kindergarten, Frank could not remember a time when he hadn't worked at least two jobs to make ends meet. As soon as Hailey found a good day school for Janice, she helped out by getting a cashier's job at a supermarket.

"It had become apparent by the time of the celebration of our third anniversary over a meal of wieners, cheesy macaroni, and diet soda that we had gotten married far too young," Frank said. "But we were in love when we got married and we were determined to prove to everyone that the 'puppy love' that struck us when we were in sixth grade could last forever."

Frank had always had a knack for visiting yard and garage sales and coming home with real bargains; not just getting a good buy on an old chair for a couple of bucks, he said, but recognizing that the true value of an antique chair was really in the hundreds of dollars.

"My grandfather used to drag me along to all kinds of sales when I was a kid," Frank said. "He had been in the import/export business in Italy before World War II. I guess our family had once been pretty well off until a couple of bombers mistakenly dropped their payload on our warehouses instead of one of Mussolini's munitions factories. Anyway, Poppa taught me a lot about the value of everything from bottles to bootstraps."

By the time Janice started first grade and Jack was going into third, Frank had started a small antique business in an old neighborhood store that had been empty for years and that had a rent he could afford. Things started working out for them, and soon Hailey could take fewer hours at the supermarket and work in the antique store so Frank only had to work one other full-time job.

On a number of occasions when Frank was in the store, an older gentleman came in who, judging from his clothing and the expensive automobile parked outside on the street, was quite wealthy. It wasn't long before Anthony had introduced himself and had become a regular customer in the store.

"Tony loved to bargain," Frank said. "His manner was brusque, sometimes downright rude and insulting, but he always ended up paying a fair price for whatever he bought."

One afternoon when Frank arrived at the store, Hailey was almost beside herself with excitement. Tony had left her with a message for her husband: He wanted to meet Frank for lunch the next day at 12:45 P.M. He had a proposition for him.

"Tony said that it was time for us to move uptown and have a better store," Hailey said. "Honey, I think that he wants to invest in the business."

Frank studied the business card that Tony had left with Hailey. "I had always just enjoyed jousting with the guy," Frank said. "I never thought of checking him out. I knew that Tony had to have some money, but I never thought that he might have enough squirreled away at his age to be able to invest in our business."

That night, Frank made a few telephone calls and learned that Anthony was more than able to invest in anything he wished. But one of Frank's confidants emphasized that old Tony had a few idiosyncrasies, one of which was that no one should ever keep him waiting. If Tony had set a meeting for 12:45, that didn't mean one minute later. If Frank was late, his friend advised him, forget about it. Any deal that Tony might have proposed would be null and void.

The next morning, as she was getting the kids ready for school, Hailey slipped on a puddle of spilled orange juice and severely wrenched her back.

"I had to get the kids off and get Hailey to bed at the same time," Frank said. "Hailey absolutely could not move, and she would be unable to put in any time at either the supermarket or the store that day."

Frank called Hailey's mother, but she answered the telephone with a hoarse whisper, explaining that she had a terrible cold and couldn't help.

His next call was to his sister, whose answering machine informed him that she was out of town visiting friends.

The store would have to be closed for the day. The important thing was that he keep his appointment with Tony and that he be on time.

Tony lived in an upscale apartment building with a great view of the park and the river. Understandably, for his convenience, Tony had made reservations at an uptown restaurant that existed only in legend for Frank.

Frank was making good time, moving along right on schedule, when he was suddenly caught in the middle of what he decided had to be the worst traffic jam in the history of the city. After half an hour of futile honking, ineffective shouting, and bumper-to-bumper, inch-by-inch movement, Frank's one-thousandth glance at his wrist watch told him that there was no way that he would be at Tony's favorite restaurant by 12:45.

"It was 1987," Frank said. "There were no cell phones to stick in your pockets. The car phones being used at that time were far too expensive for me to afford. I couldn't call the restaurant and try to buy time from Tony. I couldn't call Hailey and ask her to scream past her pain and try to gain sympathy for my being stuck in traffic. And if Tony should call the store and ask where I was, I couldn't afford an answering service. I couldn't even afford an answering machine. I concluded that I had had it. The deal was off the table."

Frank sighed in defeat. "What the hey, I figured, you can't mourn what you never had."

But Frank knew that he really wanted the offer that it seemed Tony was going to make.

"I knew that Hailey and the kids and I hadn't been as faithful churchgoers as we could have been," Frank said. "I hadn't been to confession since I couldn't remember when. But I really started to pray for God's help. It wasn't one of these cheap kind of bargaining prayers. You know, like if you let this happen for me, I'll never ever use your name in vain again. It was just a gut-honest prayer for help . . . with a kind of a general promise that I would do my best to try to be a better person."

When Frank arrived at the restaurant at 1:05, the maitre d' showed him immediately to Tony's table.

"The guy is all smiles and tells me to sit down," Frank said. "He's taken the liberty of ordering an appetizer and he hopes that I'm not too worn out from the exasperating trauma of a traffic jam."

Frank remembers sitting down as if he were in a trance. When Tony finished telling him what had taken place, Frank was certain that he was in a trance.

About 12:40, Tony said, Frank's secretary had called and explained that Frank was in the worst traffic jam imaginable and that he might be a few minutes late.

"Wherever did you find such a charming young lady?" Tony asked Frank. "Her voice was so pleasant, completely captivating, almost musical. In spite of her charm, I did get a bit grumpy when I heard that you were going to be late for whatever reason, but she soon had me laughing at one of her clever jokes.

What an asset she will be when you move your business to the uptown building that I have found for you. I know you and your wife are going to love it."

Frank knows that he owes his present success with the antique store to an angel.

"Who else could it have been who called Tony and sweet talked him into not being angry that I was caught in traffic and would be late for our meeting?" Frank asked. "When I got home and told Hailey about our 'secretary' and how she had saved the deal, she, too, said that it could only have been an angel who interceded for us."

Later, when the new store opened and Tony wanted to meet the charming lady with the enchanting voice, Frank and Hailey told him that they were sorry, but she was no longer with them; she had decided to return to her home, in what she had told them was a heavenly place to live.

*C*larissa of Vancouver, Washington, told us of a remarkable healing experience in which angelic beings appeared to restructure her physical body. According to her testimony, the experience changed her life.

"Before the angels visited me," Clarissa said, "I weighed 300 pounds. I was fat, ugly, unhealthy, unhappy, and mean to everyone I knew."

One night, she said, a voice awakened her and told her not to be frightened. Clarissa became very nervous and struggled to get out of bed. "But some unseen hands gently pushed me back down," she said. "I could see seven pillars of swirling, sparkling lights. Within moments, they assumed a general human shape, and I sensed five males and two female light beings."

Clarissa remained fearful and confused until one of the female beings touched her soothingly on the forehead and told her that they would not hurt her.

They had come in answer to her prayers, spoken and unspoken; they had come to cleanse her body.

Then, somehow, the angels lifted her spirit body, the "real Clarissa," out of her physical body. At the same time, Clarissa was faintly aware of her body lying about three feet beneath her on the bed.

As she watched in awe, the light beings began to work on her body. "At one point, it was as if they took some kind of glowing fishnet and pulled it through my physical body," she said. "They began to knead my flesh, as if it were made of some kind of dough. When they were finished, it felt as if they had opened up my ribs and pushed the 'real me' back in."

Whatever occurred that night, the angelic cleansing was highly successful. Although all previous attempts at dieting and exercise programs had ended in dismal failure, within a remarkably brief period of time, Clarissa began to shed pounds as the proverbial duck sheds water. At the time that she wrote to us in 1992, she carried a healthy 140 pounds on her five-foot-eight frame. A follow-up communication a few years later revealed that Clarissa had lost even more weight. Clarissa's attitude toward people and life in general changed from her former mean and surly stance to a cheery, always look on the bright side of life. She had also obtained a good job as a paralegal and was engaged to be married.

*W*e are certain that it has occurred to many readers of this book that a good many individuals experience contact with angels or light beings while they are undergoing an out-of-body (OBE) or near-death experience (NDE). In an OBE, individuals feel certain that their soul, or their mind, truly leaves the body during an altered state of consciousness and travels to other dimensions or other geographical locations on Earth. Many are convinced that they were accompanied by their guardian angel or spiritual guide during these out-of-body journeys.

After nearly five decades of research, we have determined what we believe to be some of the most common types of out-of-body experiences—or, one might say, situations in which OBEs might occur. In each instance, the person experiencing it may report having been guided by an angel:

1. Projections that occur while the subject sleeps

2. Projections that occur while the subject is undergoing surgery, childbirth, tooth extraction, etc.

3. Projections that occur at the time of an accident, during which the subject suffers a violent physical jolt that seems, literally, to catapult his spirit from his physical body

4. Projections that occur during intense physical pain

5. Projections that occur during acute illness

6. Projections that occur at the moment of physical death, when the deceased subject appears to a living person with whom he has had a close emotional link

7. Projections that occur during near-death experiences (NDEs), wherein the subject is revived and returned to life through heart massage or other medical means. Dr. Raymond Moody first used the term near-death experience in about 1971, and the new nomenclature replaced the previously used "pseudo-death" or "false death," which had been used to describe the experiences of those who, while apparently dead, had seen deceased relatives, tunnels of light, life reviews, angelic beings, and a sense of peace before being resuscitated.

In addition to these spontaneous, involuntary experiences that we have listed above, there are also those voluntary and conscious projections during which the subject deliberately endeavors to free his mind from his physical body.

After his friend had accidentally struck Peter in the throat, he couldn't breathe, and started gasping for breath.

"I felt myself starting to spin . . . like I was falling a long, endless fall," Peter said. "Then I was no longer spinning, no longer gasping for breath. Everything around me was the deepest, darkest, black that I had ever seen. I felt no fear at all; I felt a sense of peace that I have never felt before.

"And then there was a light in front of me. As I looked, I realized that there was no ground beneath my feet, but I saw that somehow my body was connected to the light and I continued to feel a sense of peace about me. I felt that it was so pure, so good, and so understanding, not condemning or judging. I saw the light come to a stop far below me. Where it rested, it formed a perfect circle. Then I noticed that there was a figure in the circle of light. I don't know how, but I knew that it was my physical body. As I looked down on it, I still continued to feel the same sense of peace. Then I realized that I was no longer in any kind of physical form, that I was now in the immortal form that we call 'spirit.'

"Suddenly the light was gone . . . I heard a loud, indistinguishable sound all around me. Then I felt something forcing its way into my chest, and I felt a slight pain throughout my body. I opened my eyes to find myself lying on the ground. My friend told me that I had only been on the ground for a second or two before opening my eyes."

In January of 1991, David was shot with a sawed-off, 12-gauge shotgun by three kids on a joyride looking for trouble. David was the only survivor of at least four people that the teenagers, with no respect for human life, had shot "just for fun" within a one-year period.

After falling into a dark place, David said that he opened his eyes to a terrible conscious reality: He found himself in Hell. It was as if some horrible case of mistaken identity had occurred—David was the victim, not the murderer.

"I was in that terrible place for only a brief time before two angels appeared to take me with them to Heaven," David said. "I thought the demons might not want to give me up, but there seemed to be an unspoken agreement that I had been sent to the wrong place."

Soon, David found himself standing at the River of Life, staring across the water at a great city of gold.

"I wanted to go there," he said, "But the two angels told me that I was not yet allowed to cross the river or to enter the city of gold."

The next thing David experienced was being surrounded by an intense, bright light. Although he apologizes for sounding presumptuous, he believes that he was standing before God, the source of the incredibly brilliant light.

"I was in complete fear beyond all words or human understanding," David said. "Yet, at the same time, there was also a feeling of peace beyond all human understanding. I wanted to stay, but the two angels told me that I could not remain there; it was not yet my time."

After recovering from his wounds, David said that he had been searching for anything that might compare, in even the smallest way, to the peace that he experienced in the company of the angels. "But I know in my heart," he explained, "that I will not find such peace again until it is my time."

*C*onnor had just finished a week of tough tests before Christmas vacation. It was his senior year in college, and he needed the best grades he could squeeze out to pave a smoother path for graduate school. There had also been a couple of somewhat excessive holiday parties with his friends and a rather emotional goodbye scene with the girl he had just begun dating.

"I was really looking forward to getting home and sleeping for at least three days," he said. "Of course, I realized there would be fat chance of that happening, because I knew Dad would want me to help out in the mailing and packing store that he managed. The holiday season was the busiest time of the year by far. Mom would be working there, and so would my younger sister, a high school senior."

Connor was beginning to regret very deeply the late-night study and party sessions before his long drive home, when he swerved to avoid hitting a deer that wasn't there. Connor was succumbing to a kind of highway hypnosis that was causing him to see things that weren't real.

"It was just getting dark," he said. "I was driving in a forested area that had signs posted every few miles to warn motorists of deer crossings.

"I had swerved to avoid hitting a family of deer that turned out to be a clump of rural-route mailboxes."

Wisdom dictated that he should find a rest area and catch a nap, but he didn't want to take the time. If he kept driving—allowing for a stop for some strong coffee and a sandwich—he should arrive home around two o'clock in the morning.

Connor pulled off the highway at the very next exit he saw proclaiming gas, food, and lodging. He didn't yet need gas, and lodging was out of the question if he was to maintain his arrival schedule, but it was time to get some caloric energy and caffeine.

Although he was not really a coffee drinker, Connor ordered two cups as black and strong as his taste buds could tolerate, to wash down the overdone hamburger. Prior experience reminded him that too much coffee only made for more comfort stops, and, thus, more time spent on the road.

After two hours of driving, Connor once again found himself nodding off. He opened the window on the driver's side, letting some cool air into the vehicle to help keep him awake.

"And then I was pulling into the driveway at home," Connor said. "Mom, Dad, and Sis were already in bed. I would just slip in quietly and bring in my luggage in the morning. Within minutes I was beneath the covers and just beginning to fall asleep."

"*Connor! Wake up, Connor! Wake up!*"

"Jeez, Dad," Connor complained. "Let me catch a few more z's, won't you? C'mon, it's my first day of vacation."

And then, Connor jerked awake, his senses muddled.

He wasn't at home and in bed: He was still in his car—and heading for an embankment.

Connor pulled over to the side of the road and got out of the car. He walked around his vehicle, then did a few jumping jacks to wake up. After a few minutes of calisthenics, he convinced himself that he was ready to safely drive the final ninety minutes home.

"It was probably twenty minutes later," Connor said, "that in my altered state of consciousness, I was hugging my girlfriend and promising her that I would call her often over the holidays. I might have been making that telephone call from the Other Side if at that very moment, I hadn't felt two very strong and rough hands grab me by the shoulders and shake me into full wakefulness."

Connor was startled into complete consciousness. The physicality of the hands had been so strong that he was convinced that someone had got into the backseat of his car when he had stopped to do some calisthenics at the side of the road.

"I pulled over and turned on all the interior lights," Connor said. "There was no one in the backseat. Of course, I had really known that before I turned on the lights. I was now so wide awake with the adrenaline pumping through my veins that I had no trouble with any nodding off before I pulled into the driveway of my family home."

The next morning when his family greeted him, Connor told them just how wonderful a Christmas it truly was: His guardian angel had made certain that he arrived home safely. A guardian angel, he added, with some really strong hands.

*W*hile picking up a few snacks in a convenience store late at night with her friend Chloe, Alyssa suddenly received a message from her guardian angel warning that they were being stalked.

"Ever since I was a little girl," Alyssa said, "I would get these warnings inside my head from my guardian angel whenever any kind of trouble or danger was near. Chloe has been my best friend since second grade, and now that we are in our twenties, she has witnessed enough times when my angel has protected me that she doesn't argue whenever I get a danger signal."

Alyssa said that she leaned toward Chloe and whispered that Skywalker was telling them to get out of there.

"I had nicknamed my angel Skywalker after Luke in *Star Wars*," Alyssa explained. "I figured that since an angel's home is somewhere way up in the sky, that that was a good name."

Chloe motioned with a jerk of her head toward a well-dressed man in a gray raincoat by the beer cooler who was watching them with more than casual interest. Thanks to the angelic warning, Alyssa and Chloe quickly picked out their snacks and began to walk toward the cashier to pay for their items.

The stranger in the raincoat stepped in front of them, blocking their exit, and asked them if they would like a ride home.

"I had been to this convenience store before late at night. On those occasions it was full of folks," Alyssa said. "Wouldn't you know that just when we need a bunch of heroes, the place is empty except for the skinny kid behind the cashier's counter."

Alyssa and Chloe declined the man's offer and asked to be allowed to continue to the cashier.

Without another word, the man grabbed Alyssa and began dragging her toward the back of the store. Chloe struck him with a large bottle of beer and the man fell on the floor.

"He cursed, reached behind his head, and saw that Chloe had drawn blood," Alyssa said. "Now he was really mad, and he started to get up, making certain that we knew, in the most coarse kind of language, what he was going to do to us."

Before their assailant could regain his feet, a man who must have been somewhere in the store unnoticed, picked up the man, dragged him to the door, and threw him outside. The frightened and startled predator struggled to his feet and ran to his vehicle. Within seconds, he had disappeared into the late-night traffic.

Alyssa and Chloe thanked their hero for saving them. "He was a fairly tall man," she recalls, "but he was really slender, almost slight in appearance. He surely didn't look strong enough to have picked that big lug up and thrown him out of the store."

The man nodded quietly in response to their expressions of gratitude, then walked to the door. Just before he stepped outside, he said in a very soft voice, "You two shouldn't be out so late at night."

Alyssa and Chloe paid for their snacks, and noticed that their intercessor was still sitting in his car with the motor running.

"It was obvious to us that he wanted to see that we got out of that neighborhood safely and to be certain that our assailant didn't come back," Alyssa said. "He followed us as we drove away from the store and until we got back on the main highway."

Alyssa said that a few days later, a police officer came to her apartment complex to ask her to identify a photo of the man who had attempted to assault them in the convenience store. Chloe was visiting her with her two young children, so the officer was pleased that he could get her identification at the same time.

"It was the guy, all right," Alyssa said. "The police had found the creep; there was no doubt. It turned out that he was a known sexual predator and that he had a history of violence."

The police officer told Alyssa and Chloe that they had been very fortunate to get away from their assailant before he managed to get either one, or both, of them into his car.

"There was no luck involved," Alyssa told the officer. "A real hero came to our rescue, picked the creep up, and threw him out the door. What about him, did you get his name? We would sure like to thank him."

The police officer looked at the two women, frowning his puzzlement. "What man?" he asked them.

Alyssa and Chloe, sometimes excitedly speaking over one another, described the good citizen who had interceded on their behalf, and thrown the would-be predator out of the store.

After listening in baffled silence to their testimony, the police officer told them that the cashier hadn't mentioned any man who had come to their rescue.

Chloe protested that the young man had probably been so frightened by the attack that he had hidden under the counter and not really seen anything.

The police officer told them that there was an easy way to settle this extremely bizarre dispute. In case it might be necessary to aid in the identification of the perpetrator, he had brought along a copy of the convenience store's security tape. Removing it from his briefcase, the office inserted the tape into Alyssa's VCR.

To their astonishment, Alyssa and Chloe watched the footage and saw the stalker grab Alyssa and begin to pull her toward the back of the store. Fighting back to protect her friend, Chloe struck him with the bottle. He fell to the floor, struggled to his feet, then ran out the door. There was not a single image of the tall, slender man who had come to their rescue.

Alyssa looked at Chloe, smiled broadly, then whispered, "It was Skywalker."

Chloe nodded in agreement. "After all these years, you finally saw what he looks like."

Alyssa had tears running down her cheeks. "And I got to see my guardian angel together with my best friend; My Earth friend and my heavenly friend."

The police officer had their testimony regarding the perpetrator's identity, and he quietly decided that the conversation had taken a turn beyond his jurisdiction. As he rose and thanked them for their cooperation, he added, "The important thing was that neither of you two ladies were injured by this monster."

Alyssa agreed, then added that they were fortunate that there was an angel on duty that night.

Martha told us of the time she was a single mom out of a job whose unemployment insurance had just run out. Although her situation seemed desperate, her guardian angel provided for her in a unique way.

"I grew up in Missouri, and my dad always said we were dirt poor, but proud," Martha said. "He managed to eke out a living on his homestead of 160 acres, and was able to feed and clothe a wife, four kids, and two 'coon hounds. We might not have had the best of clothes and drove the newest car, but there was always enough food on the table so that no one ever went to bed hungry. And we always went to church every Sunday—even if the boys wore their bib overalls and we girls wore dresses made out of cloth feed sacks."

After graduating from high school in 1997, Martha had continued to work in a local supermarket as a cashier until she had enough money set aside to enroll in business college in a nearby city. There she had met Kevin, a high school English teacher, who was active in a little theater group. Martha had always loved to sing, so it didn't take much urging on Kevin's part to convince her to try out for a part in their production of *Bye Bye Birdie*. To her astonishment and delight, she won the role of Kim, the high school girl infatuated with Conrad Birdie, the character loosely based on Elvis Presley; and to no one's surprise, Kevin got the part of Conrad, the singer with the hypnotic charisma and a massive ego.

It was a difficult but exhilarating six weeks of late-night rehearsals at the theater and early morning classes at the business college. Martha's singing easily won her fellow thespians' approval, but the choreographer, a fussy martinet who claimed Broadway credentials, found her dancing skills sadly lacking. Martha hadn't realized just how many exhausting dance routines featured her character. While others went home to get some rest, Martha had to stay after rehearsal to work on her moves. For a week before the play opened, the choreographer had her coming in early, before rehearsals and the others arrived.

"Ever since my mother told me as a little girl that I had a guardian angel watching over me, I had from time to time asked that benevolent being for its help in one thing or another," Martha said. "With all my might, I asked my angel to grant me some heavenly grace to move my feet and body with the music and not against it. I know it was with my angel's help that on opening night I got a standing ovation after one dance number."

In retrospect, Martha believes that it was a combination of the romance of the theater and complete physical and mental exhaustion that contributed to her accepting Kevin's proposal of marriage a few days after the musical's run ended. It was June, Kevin decreed, the perfect month to be a bride, and school was over for the summer.

"It all happened in a blur," she said. "We were married after being engaged for barely a month. After a wonderful honeymoon in the Ozarks, I expected to settle back to taking classes at the business college, and Kevin would teach remedial reading until school began in September."

But Kevin had other ideas. He had always wanted to be an actor, he told Martha. He had only taken a teaching job until he felt the time was right to open his wings and fly. The applause of the audience each night as he strutted across the stage as Conrad Birdie had convinced him that it was time for him to go to New York and realize his passion.

Martha tried to reason with her husband, pointing out that the approval of a hometown audience and the encouragement of a director who was also the music teacher at the high school was not quite the same as winning the acceptance of an experienced Broadway director and an audience of sophisticated theatergoers.

"Kevin accused me of trying to burst his bubble," Martha said. "He begged me to support him in his dream. He had it all planned, that I could work as a secretary while he tried out for parts in plays and musicals. He told me that he had always seen himself on Broadway. He just knew that he could make it. Broadway was always looking for fresh talent."

And so, they left for New York, found an apartment that Martha said was little more than a closet with hot and cold running cockroaches, and Kevin began to make the rounds of theatrical agents' offices and theater tryouts. He did convince an agent to represent him, and Martha managed to get a secretarial job that kept them from starvation—until she got pregnant with Joey.

Martha asked her angel for strength to become a good mother, and she added a prayer that now that he was going to be a father, Kevin would abandon his futile dream of success on the Broadway stage and return home to Missouri.

"But Kevin was shocked, angry, confused, and wanted to know why such a thing had happened to us," Martha said. "I asked him if he had ever taken a sex-education class; pregnancy was not something I had developed spontaneously on my own."

Martha worked at her job with the understanding that she would have to leave once her extended size presented an obstacle in the office. When that day arrived early in her ninth month, Kevin had managed to get employment as a waiter in one of the show-business hangouts where he had been a regular. A friend of Kevin's, who had been pursuing his own dream of seeing his name up in lights far longer than Kevin, assured him that working as a waiter in this particular restaurant was a great way to get noticed by directors and producers.

Once Martha came home with baby Joey, she didn't see much of Kevin.

"He stopped by to pay the rent and to give me a little money now and then," Martha said. "He didn't seem to want to know his own son. He would lean over the crib, do the same stupid 'coochy-coochy-coo' routine, then leave, saying that he had a lead on a part in an off-Broadway play or that he was late to work or some other excuse to get out of there as fast as possible."

This steady pattern of indifference continued for over a year. Martha had been able to get her secretary job back, but after a few months, her boss had to let her go because of her inability to find a dependable, steady babysitter for Joey, and, consequently, missing too many days of work.

Martha said that she was not surprised the night Kevin came by to inform her that he wanted a divorce. He told her that he had fallen in love with a young actress who really understood him and his need to pursue his passion for the stage. Further, he explained, he couldn't really afford to pay any child support, but he would stop by from time to time to give Martha and Joey what he could. He was, after all, a man who honored his obligations.

"That night I prayed so hard to my guardian angel that I think my neighbors heard me through those thin walls of the apartment," Martha said. "Since childhood, I had only prayed silently or maybe with just a little whisper, but that night, I prayed out loud, desperately."

For another couple of weeks, Martha tried to hang on to the hope that somehow, some miracle would occur; but it seemed that things only got darker. She knew that her family back in Missouri couldn't help. Their fortunes had never prospered; they still managed to just hang on. And Kevin's irregular child-support payments barely allowed her to buy food for Joey. Martha knew that unless she made the overdue rent payment to her landlord very soon, she would be turned out onto the streets.

"I know I sat in front of the telephone book an hour before I opened it," she said. "I could hear my father's voice inside my head, reminding me that our family never asked anybody for help, ever, but I also knew that I was in a desperate situation. I did need help, and I couldn't just grow some vegetables or grab some eggs from the henhouse. I decided to call the Welfare offices."

Martha knows that she correctly copied down the telephone number and slowly, carefully punched each number. She was puzzled when the woman who answered the telephone on the other end identified herself as the personnel director of a large business firm.

Before Martha could explain that she was calling Welfare, the woman was itemizing the qualifications that the applicant who wished the job must possess. Martha pushed back her astonishment and responded to the list of requirements by affirming that she did, indeed, possess all of the needed skills.

The personnel director seemed satisfied and told Martha that she should appear for an appointment early the next morning. "Of course, I will make my final decision after our in-person meeting," she advised Martha, "but you certainly sound perfect for the position."

Martha's neighbor watched Joey while she went to apply for the job at the well-established business firm. She and the personnel director developed an immediate rapport, and Martha was hired for the position.

"As I was leaving the office," Martha said, "the woman remarked how relieved she was to find someone so qualified so quickly. It seems that she had called an employment agency to express their emergency need for a very special someone who could fill the vacant position immediately. I had called less than an hour after she had placed the call."

Martha said that the position turned out to be her dream job, with a salary and benefits that soon enabled her to obtain a larger apartment and to afford a wonderful day school for Joey.

"I never told anyone at the office that I had been calling the Welfare Agency and got their number by mistake," Martha said, "because I know that it was no mistake: My guardian angel had punched just exactly the right numbers."

$\mathcal{A}$l said that he was born at 4:02 A.M. in Jersey City, New Jersey. His mother and father were on the way to the hospital when they were hit head-on by another car. His father suffered two broken legs, and his mother's injuries were far worse.

"Mother was literally 'broken' from the waist down and from the sternum up," Al said. "Mother was given last rites at the scene, since it appeared highly doubtful that she would live long enough to reach the emergency room. My birth was called a miracle by the attending doctors and nurses. Mother spent the next seventeen months in the hospital, and I was raised at that time by my grandmother."

Exactly one year later, with his mother still in the hospital, Al was in a bassinet in his grandmother's house.

"I have been told that it was a beautiful fall evening," Al said. "The windows were open, and my grandmother had placed a lighted religious candle on a dresser. The wind kicked up, and the shear drapes billowed out until they touched the candle's flickering flame long enough to catch fire."

It didn't take long for the entire house to catch fire, and, of course, since Al's room was the area where the fire had begun, it was completely engulfed in flames.

What happened next was declared a miracle, the second in little Al's life, and the local newspapers and television stations featured an interview with the fire-man who rescued him from the inferno. The heroic firefighter told the media that angels had saved the baby from a terrible death by fire. He had entered the room and been astounded to see two angels protect-ing the baby. As if witnessing such an angelic visita-tion were not remarkable enough, one of the angels had picked up the child and handed it to him.

Years later, Al managed to speak with the fireman who rescued him and to hear for himself his testimony.

"He said that he could not believe his eyes when he entered my room," Al stated. "Through the smoke and terrible heat, two large angels were crouched over my bassinet. The fireman said that he froze for a moment, and all of a sudden one of the angels, who had a trumpet strapped to his body, picked me up and handed me to him. The fireman was able to escape from the fire without getting a scratch on me or before I had suffered from smoke inhalation."

*B*ridget developed an interest in spirituality at a very young age. At that particular time, her parents did not attend any religious services, but her mother granted her wishes by taking her to a nearby place of worship. When Bridget was ten, she asked God to come into her heart.

Bridget began to experience prophetic dreams and visions, such as the ones in which she escorted the souls of children into Heaven. In her dreams, she would enter the rooms where children lay dying, comfort them, and accompany them to a higher world.

A few years ago, as an adult driving to work on a busy expressway on a rainy morning, she experienced angelic intervention.

"A car swerved into my lane," Bridget said. "I applied the brake to keep from hitting the intruder. When I did so, my vehicle skidded out of control. A pickup truck hit my vehicle as I slid toward the median."

When the "demolition" was over, she saw the front of the truck—it was distorted, and broken glass was scattered across the blacktop. Bridget's first fear was that the driver of the truck had been killed.

Remarkably, she could get out of her own battered vehicle, and once she was free, she ran to the truck and saw that the driver, a young man, was also okay.

As she stood in the road, trying to pull herself together, a middle-aged man said to her, "I saw the accident. I stopped the traffic so that you and the other driver would not be hit again." The man pointed to his white car, which signaled other drivers to slow down.

Bridget immediately walked toward the truck driver, saying, "Wasn't it nice of that man to stop and help us like that? He risked his own vehicle and his safety to help us."

The young man looked confused and asked, "What man?"

Bridget whirled around and saw that the Good Samaritan had vanished. Where his car had been just moments before, a police car with flashing lights now warned motorists of the accident scene.

"I believe that a guardian angel was there on the highway that day, and that God had prevented a fatality," Bridget said. "The middle-aged man's face was pleasant, and his smile reassuring. I thought later about the white car, and remembered the Bible's association with the color white and purity."

Bridget said that she is thankful to God—or the Great Spirit as her Native American ancestors called Him—for all the help that He has given her and her loved ones. "I have told Him that my spiritual 'antenna' is fully extended, so that I may receive all the messages that He is willing to give me."

*A*mong the shamanic teachings of the traditional Native Americans, the totem animal represents the physical form of one's spirit helper, the guide, the guardian. Contrary to the misinterpretations of early missionaries, the native people did not worship these animal representations of their guides as gods.

Those who follow the spiritual path of the traditional ways believe in a total partnership with the world of spirits and the ability to make personal contact with individual spirit guides and guardians. The spirit guide, and its totem animal representation, is obtained when the youthful supplicant embarks on his or her vision quest.

The spirit guides, appearing as totemic animals, guide people to the mysterious, transcendent reality beyond the material world and take them into another dimension of time and space where the inhabitants of the spirit world dwell. It is through such a portal that traditional shamans must pass to gain their contact with the benevolent beings—the grandfathers and grandmothers—who reside there. With their spirit guide at their side in the form of a totem animal, it is possible to communicate with the spirits and derive wisdom and knowledge.

Dr. Walter Houston Clark wrote of the occasions when he personally explored the mystical consciousness in various Native American rituals, and concluded that those individuals who received messages from angels or sacred figures in dreams or visions should treat these beings with respect.

Traditional followers of Native American spiritual practices certainly treat their guardian spirits with respect, and they use the information given to them as lessons about themselves to be used in the most effective performance of their beliefs.

$\mathcal{A}$bby had worked late at her Denver office, and when she finally left a few minutes after ten o'clock, she became aware that she was being followed to the parking lot by two men.

"My husband always worried when I worked late because there was an after-hours bar that was not that far from the office," Abby said. "I promised him that I would never walk to the parking lot alone, that I would see that one of the fellows escorted me to my car. The problem on this night was that the rest of the staff had left hours before me."

Abby kept a steady pace until she reached her parked vehicle. Just as she was reaching out to place the key in the door lock, one of the men grabbed her wrist.

"Don't be in such a hurry," he grinned lecherously. "The party hasn't even started yet."

The other man moved in closer and said that they would take his car and leave hers in the parking

225

lot. He promised to bring her back to her car after the party was over.

The next sound the two men heard was that a very loud, menacing growl.

"What the blazes is that?" the taller man wondered, moving to stand behind his shorter, but heavier, friend.

Moving with powerful grace from the shadows, there appeared a very large, white German shepherd or wolf. Its eyes seemed to have a reddish glow to them as the canine curled back its muzzle to display long, sharp teeth.

"Hey, pooch!" the taller man shouted, affecting a show of bravado. "Run along home. Beat it! Nobody wants you here!"

"Oh, I do," Abby said, speaking for the first time. "I want White Wolf here with me."

"Is . . . is that your dog?" the men wanted to know.

"It belongs to my husband," she answered.

"Will . . . will he bite?" one of the men asked.

"Horribly," Abby smiled. "Voraciously."

The men kept nervous eyes on the white wolf as they cautiously backed away.

Within moments, the two male predators had disappeared—and when Abby looked back toward the car, so had the great white wolf.

Abby said that this wasn't the first time the massive wolf had appeared to help her when she was in danger. She explained that her husband was of Native American heritage, and followed, as much as possible, the traditional ways of his tribe. Whenever he felt that Abby was in trouble, he prayed for her protection and asked for help from the wolf, his totem animal.

"To my husband," Abby said, "his totem animal is like what many of us would call a guardian angel."

"hey say that God doesn't give you more than you can handle," Priscilla Garduno Wolf commented wryly, quoting an oft-repeated mantra of positive thinking. "Well, I had seriously begun to question if that was really true."

Priscilla's husband had deserted her and their five-month-old son, Erik, after he found out that she had cancer. The marriage had been rocky for about a year, and the mental abuse had grown worse. Then, he left them to survive as best they could on their own.

"I kept telling myself that God removes all the bad if you have faith," Priscilla said, "but then I lost my home and my teenage daughter began having problems. It was hard to support a family and keep it together."

Priscilla had always believed that everything happens for a reason. That we learn from our mistakes.

"However, when you learn that you have cancer and are facing many hardships, it does make you wonder where God is," she said. "Why had God forsaken me?"

One day, several weeks after her husband had deserted the family, and she was lying in bed in great pain, Priscilla could hear her baby crying for her. "My baby kept calling out, 'Mama! Mama!' I felt so helpless—I couldn't move, yet my son needed me," Priscilla recalled.

Erik crawled to her bedroom door with his empty bottle in his hand—then he stood up, like someone was lifting him.

"There was a bright flash, and a heavenly light surrounded my son," Priscilla said. "I could see the form of a man, and I knew he was my son's spiritual guide."

The angelic spirit began to walk away from her, and Erik started to move his hand, calling her to follow.

"Get up," the spirit guide said, turning to look sternly at Priscilla. "There's nothing wrong with you!"

Priscilla forced herself to get up and walk slowly toward the angel and her son.

"As I struggled in the hallway, it seemed like a million miles away to the kitchen," she said. "I fixed my son's bottle, then I dragged myself to the sofa, grabbed the diaper bag, and changed him. He was so happy; he kept kissing me. Later, I managed to walk back to the kitchen, pulled myself up to the kitchen sink, and drank water like I was a dried-up river full of dirt. I felt the water inside me—and then I felt a touch of life within me. That was when the spirit guide left us."

Within a week, Priscilla said, she had been healed by the angel who had visited them.

Today, Priscilla Garduno Wolf is a well-known Native American artist, storyteller, and *curandera* ("healer"), affectionately known to her friends by her Apache name, Little Butterfly.

"The Great Spirit has been there for me," Priscilla said. "I have been sick and recovered. I have raised my son until adulthood, and now he has children of his own."

At the age of ten, after having lived harmoniously with nature in an isolated wooded area surrounded by five lakes, Sunny was taken away from her tribal family and the Shawnee traditional way of life to attend the white man's school.

"After that," she said, "I was punished if I 'acted like an Indian' or spoke my language. Because of this, I did not do my vision quest at the usual age of around twelve."

Sunny's life became "many years of confusion, abuse, and survival." It wasn't until her children were grown and she had endured years of alcoholism that she had a spiritual experience that ended her addiction and placed her feet on a spiritual path.

On January 23, 1984, after a ten-day drinking binge, a female-elder spirit appeared to Sunny when she was, literally, at the point of death; she had eaten nothing and had had little water for ten days.

The image of the elder spirit communicated telepathically with her, and Sunny remembered that she was given a choice: "To walk on into death or to follow the purpose that I had come to Earth to do. The choice I made is obvious.

"There was only an apple in the house to eat, and I remember crawling to the refrigerator to get it. As I ate, sparkles of light like fireflies seemed to be all around me before they entered my skin. My energy slowly returned, and I was cured of my alcohol addiction."

Sunny said that the elder spirit became a part of her. "She stayed with me until 1992, when I was sixty-one and disobeyed a direct instruction by a spirit being who came to me as a deer," Sunny said. "At that time, all spirit contact withdrew from me."

The knowledge that her disobedience had caused the withdrawal of vital spirit contact so devastated Sunny that she began preparing for a vision quest.

In October 1992, she spent four days and nights at Big Sur, California, crying for her purpose and asking how she might best help her people. She wanted to know how she could best help accomplish the unity and harmony of American Indian peoples.

On the fourth day, three crows came to sit on rocks in the Big Sur River just in front of her. They looked straight at her, and she wondered what message they had for her.

Then they all flew up together and showed her a red-tailed hawk that was circling a tiny rainbow in the sky. This tiny rainbow appeared in no scientific relation to sun or rain.

The hawk circled the rainbow four times as Sunny watched in awe. "I knew this was the vision I had cried for," she declared. "As I watched, the tiny rainbow turned to a rosy hue, and a very powerful energy filled me with overwhelming love."

She knew then that she and her spirit guide were one in the energy.

In the days that followed, she was given the knowledge that she had received a new name, Chobeka-sepe (Medicine River), and that she was to create a newsletter for Native American prison inmates. Her mother had passed away to the Spirit World two years before, and had left a small bequest to "help people anyway you can." This seemed like the best use of her mother's bequest. But while Sunny was a writer and had distributed a small family newsletter, she had no idea where to begin such a large undertaking. She had never given a thought to prison inmates in her life.

"All the necessary information came to me when I needed it," she said, "and six weeks later, in December 1992, our first newsletter went out to about 150 people all over the world. The name *Earthbridge* came to me in a flash of insight. Such insights are not entirely physical or mental, but both, and certain knowledge."

Since October 17, 1992, Sunny Chobeka-Sepe's life has been consumed by the *Earthbridge Circle*. Soon, over 500 prison inmates and supporters all over the world called *Earthbridge Circle* their family.

"I always know that I can go back to the source of energy and love by returning to the vision of the rosy glow of my spirit guide," Sunny said. "When I am refilled with love-energy to overflowing, I must then give it out to all who wish to receive."

Earthbridge Circle grew to include friends in Belgium, France, Germany, Spain, Netherlands, Norway, Italy, England, Ireland, Canada, Switzerland, Australia, and Japan—all working toward bringing back the spiritual and cultural ways of the American Indian.

When Helen brought her daughter, Joy, to see Dr. J. C. Hugh MacKimmie, the young girl was on crutches, with ice bags packed all around her right lower leg and foot. Eleven years old, Joy's strange and mysterious foot pain had gotten so bad that she could not put any weight on her foot, and it had to be kept nearly frozen with ice at all times to relieve her suffering.

Helen told Dr. MacKimmie that Joy was tired all of the time and spent most of her time in bed. The previous doctors and specialists who had examined Joy were mystified by her illness, and their various treatments had not helped her condition.

Helen took her daughter's crutches and removed the ice packs, and she and Dr. MacKimmie helped Joy sit up on the treating table. Joy's feet dangled off the table. Even with no weight on her foot, it was obvious to Dr. MacKimmie that Joy was in terrible pain.

Dr. MacKimmie asked why Helen had brought her daughter to see him.

Nervous silence filled the room. Helen crossed the room and sat down on a chair facing him. Dr. MacKimmie could see that she was uncomfortable. She looked as if she would rather do anything else than answer him.

When he pursued the subject, Helen's face flushed. She stammered that it was all because of advice received during prayer. An inner voice, intuition, or guidance had instructed her to make an appointment with him. At first, Helen was undecided by the manner in which the instructions were received, but when her husband, Jerry, said there was no way for them to go on vacation with Joy on crutches, she finally decided they had nothing to lose by seeing him. She called for an appointment, and here they were, hoping to get help for Joy.

Dr. MacKimmie smiled and said, "The ways of the Universe are exceedingly mysterious and extraordinary."

On the day that Helen brought her daughter Joy to see him, Dr. MacKimmie was aware of angels joining them, gathering around them to form a powerful circle of light.

"Shimmering rainbow colors flowed around these heavenly beings, while bright, shining ribbons of this light reached out to touch us," Dr. MacKimmie said. "Mother and daughter were unaware of our angelic visitors or being touched by the rainbow light, but I knew a miracle was about to take place."

The angels assured him that Joy's foot problem was no problem at all, except for a few blocked energy centers in her leg. Their instructions were to run energy into her leg and foot. After a few moments, one of the radiant angelic beings said firmly, "It is done."

Dr. MacKimmie asked Joy how her foot felt. She said excitedly that it didn't hurt at all. He told Joy to put her foot down on the floor. She insisted that she couldn't, but he told her that she could now walk across the room to her mother because her foot was healed.

Joy was visibly frightened to step off the table and place any weight on her foot. Afraid to be in agony again, she refused to move an inch.

The same commanding angel ordered Dr. MacKimmie to give Joy a gentle push from behind to move her off the table. He took a deep breath and pushed the girl forward, so that she had to step on her foot as she went off the table.

Her mother cried out, "Joy, did that hurt?"

Joy shook her head and walked to Helen without using crutches. Helen and Joy were stunned.

When they left Dr. MacKimmie's office, they were rejoicing and laughing about the odd events that had brought them to him for a healing miracle.

Several days later when they returned to his office, Helen happily informed him that Joy had played tennis for two hours after they got home.

"Joy's foot never again gave her any trouble," Dr. Mackimmie said. "It has now been years later, and Helen, Joy, and I continue to marvel at how the angels brought us all together for a miraculous healing."

Dr. MacKimmie is the author of *Presence of Angels: A Healer's Life*, and is an internationally known intuitive healer who has worked with the angelic realm for more than fifty years. After graduating from the Los Angeles College of Chiropractic (now Southern California University of Health Sciences) in 1952, Dr. MacKimmie had three angels appear to him and reveal his destiny as a healer. On that fateful day, his world and its reality changed forever.

"These three angels became beloved companions, guides, and teachers," Dr. MacKimmie said, "and I have lived in their wisdom all my life. Nothing in my life is otherwise, and all else falls away. I never needed any proof or investigation, for I have always felt their heavenly presence around me. With the presence of angels, miracles can flow in healing. They, too, follow higher instruction when the Source of All Life brings us together in what are sometimes extraordinary circumstances."

When he is asked how he employs angelic energy, Dr. MacKimmie says that an angel once explained it as a heavenly exchange system in which he serves as a transmitter of angelic energies of healing and awakening for others. Whenever he raises his hands, the healing energy flows effortlessly and lovingly through him from the angelic realm to those in need. In this way, he serves as a conduit for healing and shifting soul patterns.

Currently residing in Montana with his wife, Andrea, and their two cats, Dr. MacKimmie continues to write and to work with angelic healing energies.

lthough physically fit and in good health, twenty-year-old Ethan was in a "really dark place" in his spiritual life.

"I was eating all the right foods, and I would run or walk for a couple of hours a day," he said, "but all was not right in my world. I was experiencing a kind of spiritual void."

Ethan had never been a religious person. Neither of his parents came from a church background, but they felt it was important that their son have some moral training.

"They encouraged me to attend Sunday school with our neighbors' son, a boy my age," Ethan said. "Our neighbors were hardy Methodists who never seemed to miss a single Sunday of churchgoing. I actually did go along with Ricky to Sunday school for a couple of years, and a couple of times I even attended church services with their family. I always really liked

Jesus, but as I grew older, I just couldn't go along with some of the belief concepts and certain aspects of the religion that seemed a bit too dogmatic for me."

Ethan was popular in high school and achieved a high scholastic record, as well as participated with some success in athletics. He was never a team-sports enthusiastic, but more the long-distance runner, enjoying the challenge of competing with one's own personal best in track, rather than becoming one of a group effort.

In moments of self-analysis as he began college, Ethan saw his love of running and hiking as metaphors for his wish to find his own particular path in life. By the time he was a sophomore in college, he also knew that he must choose a vocation and focus on studies that would enrich that choice.

One afternoon while hiking in a beautiful stretch of nearly untouched nature, he sat down to rest with his back against a large tree, his mind open to the wonder of the Universe.

Suddenly, Ethan was surrounded by a mysterious blue light. Feeling a moment of concern, perhaps, he will admit, even fear, he tried to see beyond the light and determine what the source of the strange illumination might be.

"That was when I perceived a commanding figure standing in the midst of the light," he said. "I have since contemplated if the figure might not have been the source of the light."

Ethan said that although no words were spoken—at least audibly—his mind was filled with images and new ways of perceiving the world around him.

"Everything around me was pulsating with light and energy," he said. "I saw that everything was alive in ways that I had never before imagined. I understood that everything was sentient. My spirit essence seemed one with all things, and I understood that life itself was far more than I had ever imagined. It seemed as though this great being was allowing me to glimpse through the dark veil that blocked human understanding of the true nature of reality."

Ethan said that the angelic teacher seemed to sense his wonder and awe, and the benevolent being smiled at him and nodded as if acknowledging that this young human had received the communication and the wisdom that had been offered to him.

"I wanted to speak, to thank this great being," Ethan said, "I wanted to express my gratitude for being allowed to glimpse beyond the physical barrier that separates us from a much greater reality. Once again, the angelic guide smiled, and I understood completely then that speech was not necessary between us. Communication had been established on a level of spirit that I had not previously deemed possible."

Ethan does not really know how long he sat against the tree after the vision of the angelic teacher had left him, but he estimates that it had to have been a couple of hours at least.

"I was not attempting to emulate Siddhartha Buddha under the Bodhi tree," he concludes his account, "and I was suddenly aware that it was becoming very cold and would soon be dark. The all-encompassing love that I had experienced definitely served to elevate my spirits and enabled me to continue life with a newfound hope and mission. I graduated in 2006 with a degree in social work, and I hope to find new ways to help those in need."

$\mathcal{O}$n April 8, 1998, Nicholas watched the SUV come through the stoplight and strike his much smaller vehicle as if it were all happening in slow motion. Nicholas doesn't think he lost consciousness for even a few seconds, and he has a clear memory of his car being pushed across the intersection and finally coming to rest against the wall of an abandoned store. The SUV had to have been traveling far in excess of the speed limit to maintain enough momentum to plow through the intersection, scraping into the sides of several other vehicles as it seemed to possess a single-minded determination to crush Nicholas's car.

Nicholas knew that he had been badly injured, but the beautiful lady who had suddenly materialized beside him spoke to him gently and kept him calm until help arrived.

"At the very first," he said, "I had no reason not to believe that the beautiful woman was a concerned passerby who had somehow managed to enter my car and sit beside me on the front seat. Although I am certain that I did not lose consciousness at any time, I was no doubt disoriented and confused. I could not feel my legs, so I knew that they were terribly injured. I was rational enough to understand that if my cheek, gashed by broken glass, hurt more than my mangled legs did, that I would not walk away from the accident."

Nicholas remembers that the woman sat beside him and assured him that everything would be all right. "She told me that although my life would change, I was up to the challenge."

When an ambulance crew, a fire truck, and a number of police cars arrived on the scene, the beautiful Good Samaritan left him.

"If I hadn't guessed her true identity of an angel before the emergency vehicles arrived, I certainly did when members of the fire department were using the Jaws of Life to extract me from my car. There was no way that anyone—anyone human—could have got in the car as crushed and crumpled as it was. I remembered that my angel was a brunette with compelling eyes, and that she was dressed in some kind of gown. It wasn't until much later that I realized the reason that I found her eyes so compelling was that somehow, when the sunlight touched her, it appeared as though her pupils were golden-hued."

Although Nicholas is thankful that he survived the crash, and feels that he adjusted to his new life without use of his legs very well, he has been confined to a wheelchair ever since his release from the hospital.

"In September 2003, my friend Jacob and I were out for a walk," Nicholas said. "Of course, this was no ordinary walk, because both Jake and I get around only by use of our wheelchairs. Jake had been a police officer and lost the use of his legs when a drug dealer had deliberately run over him. We had become good friends in physical rehab, and we enjoyed taking 'walks' whenever possible—especially in more or less off-the-beaten-path areas."

On this lovely afternoon with just a preautumn chill in the air, Nicholas and Jacob had decided to venture down a country road. They agreed that they wanted nothing to disturb or alter the quiet sanctity of the beautiful countryside, so they left their cell phones in the trunk of Jacob's car. Jake's wife and kids had a thoughtful—albeit sometimes irritating—habit of calling every fifteen minutes when they went on one of their "walks" to be certain that the two of them were all right.

Although they knew better than to attempt a gravel road, the old blacktop they chose turned out to be pretty rugged and ragged.

"By that time, thanks to the insurance money and the generosity of my family, I had an electric wheelchair," Nicholas said. "Jake got tired pretty quickly of manipulating his manual chair over the rough patches in the road, so I was towing him behind me. I knew that I couldn't keep this up for too long or I would place too great a drain on my battery."

The two friends were watching a couple of hawks circling high over head when they discovered, too late, that there was a very large pothole in the road.

"My wheels missed the huge rut, but Jake's wheels dropped into the hole, and he tipped over with his chair on top of him," Nicholas said.

Nicholas admitted that it didn't take long for despair and desperation to overwhelm the two friends. It took all of their willpower not to accuse each other of being responsible for the stupidity of deciding to toss their cell phones into the trunk.

"Jake was a big, husky man, at least 220 or more," Nicholas said. "There was no way that I could lift him, set him back on his chair, then lift the wheels out of the rut. We had been on the country blacktop for over an hour, and we hadn't seen a single car. Jake was lying in what had to have been a painfully contorted position—and he might have to stay that way for hours until someone came along."

After about twenty minutes, the two friends were relieved and elated when they saw a vintage automobile approaching. Jake, the former police officer, said that it had to be at least a 1956 model. But who cared how old the car was, as long as there was a strong man inside who could lift Jake out of the rut and place him back on his wheelchair?

"You can imagine our disappointment when the car pulled over to the side of the road and a slim young woman in blue jeans and a checkered flannel shirt stepped out onto the blacktop," Nicholas said. "That initial disappointment was soon transformed into complete astonishment, when, without uttering a word, she walked over to Jake's wheelchair and lifted it out of the rut. Then, seemingly without breaking a sweat, she bent over, grabbed Jake by the belt, and effortlessly lifted him off the blacktop, and placed him in his chair. Just before she turned to walk back to the old car in which she had arrived, she looked directly at me—and in the light from the setting sun, I saw that her pupils seemed to be of a golden hue. And then I saw the same lovely smile that had brought me so much comfort during the first minutes after my accident."

After she got into the vintage auto, the vehicle disappeared much too quickly for it to have been any ordinary car.

Jake didn't notice the rapid flight of the automobile. He was still in awe over what had just happened. "Dear God," he said, "That young Amazon acted like she knew you, Nick. Who was she?"

Nicholas nodded and admitted that he did know her. "She's my guardian angel," he answered simply.

Jake laughed at what he believed to be his friend's jest. "Well, with her around, you sure don't have to worry about a thing."

And, Nicholas confided, since that day, he never has.

*J*eremy says that he has been the conduit for numerous healings ever since he was visited by angels attired in coats of many colors when he was a teenager. As he described the process, a beautiful light became a shining, silvery fog, and then he was transported to a higher dimension.

In this otherworldly place, he found himself standing in a grassy area near a magnificent ocean. After a few moments, he became aware of a number of angels, each with a different colored robe. These benevolent beings seemed to be awaiting his arrival, for once he had become adjusted to the vibrations of the higher plane, they escorted him up the cliff, where he received teachings from angelic mentors. Jeremy said that this teaching experience repeated itself seemingly "hundreds of times."

Before he received the gift of healing when he was about sixteen, he had himself been the recipient of a number of dramatic healings. When he was an infant, he had suffered a serious case of double pneumonia, and when he was barely four, he had poked a stick into a hornets' nest and received over one hundred stings.

Jeremy commented that if he had not always lived in a state of grace, he would not have survived his early infancy.

Jeremy's sister claimed that he healed her from certain death when she accidentally became exposed to highly radioactive debris at a nuclear-waste dump.

"Kara is an activist for many causes," Jeremy said, "but this one almost cost her life. Her group discovered that nuclear waste was being illegally and irresponsibly dumped in this particular wooded area, but she made the nearly fatal mistake of wading through an actual deposit of the deadly waste. When she came to see me, her doctors had diagnosed her liver as being over 90 percent gone, and her legs were covered with melanomas. I simply put hands on her the way the angels had taught me. I can't take any credit for the process, but my sister is still alive ten years after the exposure. Her liver is nearly back to normal, and she has no melanomas."

Jeremy feels that he has become a conduit for healing energy because he has understood what his angel mentors taught him regarding the true nature of the physical body.

"We are not our bodies," he said. "Our bodies are not the source of life; they are simply a very dense structure of energy. We must never disparage our physical bodies, however, for they are the vehicles by which we receive enlightenment. Our true body, the one which we shall all inhabit one day, is the Light Body."

Jeremy says that we must all place our attention on the higher self within each of us, and the Source of All That Is—God. To assist us in attaining our cosmic purpose, there are many benevolent beings who will not desert their appointed task until humans are free of ignorance and delusion.

*I*n 1967, when she was eleven, Diana nearly drowned while swimming in the lake outside her grandparents' cabin.

"I can clearly remember sinking into the murky water of the lake," Diana said. "I had taken swimming lessons in the city in which I lived since I was four, and I had been completely confident that I could easily navigate the Michigan lake where my grandparents had their cabin. Wrong!"

Diana's swimming experience had primarily occurred in heated pools. Although it was early June, the water was quite cold, and seemed especially chilly to someone who had only waded or gone in up to her waist on previous visits to the lake.

"I really don't know what I did," Diana said. "I think my leg brushed some thick weeds or some huge fish and it startled me. I remember swallowing a lot of water, then thrashing about as if I had never taken a single swimming lesson in my life. And then I was under the water, and seemed unable to reach the surface."

That was when Diana felt strong arms around her midsection.

"Dimly, I remember seeing this young guy with long blonde hair pulling me to the surface," she said. "He seemed really strong, and he easily pulled me the twenty or so yards to shore. I can't remember if he slapped me on the back or did some artificial respiration applications, but I do vividly recall the burning in my throat as I vomited lake water and once again began to breathe normally."

As he walked away from her into the woods, the man who had rescued her seemed to become very blurred.

"Grandpa was just coming out of the cabin, and he seemed to take in all of what had just happened in the matter of a few seconds," Diana said. "I heard him shouting at the man to come back."

And then the impromptu lifeguard just seemed to disappear from view. At least that was how it seemed to Diana, who drifted into unconsciousness.

"But later, when Grandpa and Grandma were asking me questions about him, that was how it had seemed to them," Diana said. "It was as though he had just vanished into the trees and brush."

Grandpa had searched the area to thank the "long-haired man" who had saved his granddaughter, but the hero seemed to have just disappeared.

"No one recognized the description that I gave of my rescuer," Diana said. "After he pulled me to the shore, I noticed that he seemed to be wearing something like a long nightshirt. He seemed fairly tall to me, and very well built. It was the long hair that seemed to bother some of the local residents, who didn't really want any hippies or flower children camping out in the woods. I just started telling everyone that he was my guardian angel."

And that was how Diana had always described the mysterious stranger who saved her from drowning when she was a kid.

In 2006, when she was a fifty-year-old grandmother visiting her daughter and son-in-law in Dearborn, she decided to lie down for a nap in the upstairs guest room. Diana wearily decided that she wasn't used to the shrill cries in the night from a newborn grandson and the steady demands of a thirteen-month-old granddaughter.

She said that she was just getting comfortable when she became aware of a presence in the room.

"It was my guardian angel," Diana said. "The same tall, strong, long-haired 'hippie' who had saved my life when I was eleven. Now I saw clearly that the apparel that I had mistaken for a long nightshirt was a dazzling white robe."

The angel told Diana to hurry downstairs; her granddaughter was choking.

Diana said that her wonderment was broken when the angel commanded in a stern voice, "Go at once!"

Diana's son-in-law, Kyle, was watching a football game in the same downstairs room where her granddaughter sat in her playpen.

"Hannah is choking!" Diana shouted above the roar of the crowd on television.

After a quick over-the-shoulder appraisal of his daughter, Kyle said that she was mistaken; Hannah was just fine.

Diana had to concur. Hannah certainly seemed all right.

"Your granddaughter is choking!"

The angel's warning sounded within Diana's inner being with such volume that she let out a small squeal of surprise.

"Hannah is choking!" she said, raising her voice so she could not be ignored over the blaring television set.

"I thought you were going to take a nap," Kyle said, making no effort to mask his annoyance. "You must have dreamed all this. Go back upstairs and get some rest. You had a long trip and I know the kids keep you up all night. I know they sure as heck do me."

Ignoring any further assurances of Hannah's well-being, Diana leaned over the bars of the playpen and stuck her forefinger in her granddaughter's mouth. In the next instant, she pulled out a considerable portion of a rubber ear from a toy bunny. Hannah was probably seconds away from swallowing the large chunk she had managed to bite off, and it surely would have choked her to death.

Kyle was ashen-faced, and picked up his daughter to hold her to his chest. "Oh, my God, Diana, oh, my God," he said over and over.

Diana felt weak in the knees and fell back against a couch.

"I thanked God and my guardian angel for saving Hannah's life," she said. "Later, when I calmed down, I couldn't help pondering the wonder and the magnificence of the gift that had been given to me. To think that my guardian angel had first saved me when I was a child, and then saved my granddaughter from death a generation later, was such incredible proof that such benevolent beings exist and that they care about us."

Diana said that she keeps the piece of the bunny's ear in her purse as a constant reminder of the mercy and love of her angel guardian.